Praise for *Prosper*

"Ethan and Randy have developed a nearly 500-person company that has helped people all around the world find their own path to prosperity. With the action-oriented wisdom they have accumulated distilled simply in this easy-to-read book, *Prosper* is your opportunity to liberate yourself toward the work and life you've always dreamed of. I know, because they are helping me, too!"

—**Dr. Mark S. Albion, author of the *New York Times* bestseller *Making a Life, Making a Living*, Indiana University Johnson Center for Entrepreneurship and Innovation's 2010 Entrepreneur of the Year, and cofounder Net Impact**

"If you want to have your bank account, business, and relationships *prosper*—read this book!"

—**Darren Hardy, Publisher, *Success* magazine, and bestselling author of *The Compound Effect***

"The message of *Prosper* demonstrates the leadership of the authors in their commitment to helping people create the life they really want. The practical and immediately useful approach will guide people onto their path to prosperity and help them follow it!

—**Stedman Graham, Chairman and CEO, S. Graham & Associates, and bestselling author of *You Can Make It Happen* and *Teens Can Make It Happen***

"Ethan Willis and Randy Garn provide an action guide on how to achieve and sustain prosperity while finding the appropriate balance between money and happiness. Throughout the book, they offer six practices—each exemplified by entertaining and applicable stories, exercises, and insights—that help you transform your attitude and get the life you always knew you wanted."

—**Anthony Scaramucci, founder and Manager Partner, SkyBridge Capital, and author of *Goodbye Gordon Gekko***

"*Prosper* is a practical guide, detailing the concrete steps you can take to align your life with the core of your being. Follow this action plan and you'll come away with a deep understanding of what you need to be happy—and truly prosper."

—**Robert Allen, bestselling author of *Multiple Streams of Income*, *Creating Wealth*, and *Nothing Down* and coauthor of *The One Minute Millionaire***

"Ethan and Randy's book makes us recognize while we all work to prosper, few of us actually achieve *and* maintain prosperity. A great reminder to keep looking in the mirror and strive to prosper. Saddle up for a great read!"

—**Jeffrey W. Hayzlett, change agent, sometime cowboy, and author of the bestseller *The Mirror Test***

"*Prosper* is a must-read practical guidebook that will give you the inspiration to become the person you want to be."

—**Rudy Ruettiger, author, speaker, and inspiration for the 1993 movie *Rudy***

"The best book I've ever seen on how to prosper in all areas of your life. It's a masterpiece."

—**Dr. Joe Vitale, author of the international bestseller *The Attractor Factor* and the bestseller *Attract Money Now***

"This book shows you a wonderful series of strategies to help you to prosper in every area of your life, to achieve greatly in your financial life, your family relationships, your personal health, and everything you do."

—**Brian Tracy, bestselling author of *The Way to Wealth***

"Ethan and Randy are the real deal. They have perfected the business model of helping others achieve wealth and fulfillment, and this book will help you get clear on how you can create a life you love."

—**Robert Richman, cohost, Zappos Insights**

"This book will sharpen your focus and help you in business, investments, and advancement. Take a few minutes. It is worth it."

—**David Kotok, CEO, Cumberland Advisors**

"*Prosper* explains precisely how to get more of what you desire in life. Ethan Willis and Randy Garn have distilled the essence of their work into a straightforward system anyone can use to achieve more and be more."

—**Mark Sanborn, President, Sanborn & Associates, Inc., and author of *The Fred Factor* and *You Don't Need a Title to Be a Leader***

"Ethan Willis and Randy Garn have nailed it with this book! *Prosper* is a no-nonsense action guide to financial peace of mind that will help you go to the next level. Their Polaris Point concept will enable one to stay on point and achieve more than ever. Read this book and prosper!"

—**Don Hutson, CEO, U.S. Learning, Inc., and coauthor of the *New York Times* bestsellers *The One Minute Entrepreneur* and *The One Minute Negotiator***

PROSPER

PROSPER
Create the Life You Really Want

SIX PRACTICES
TO FIND LASTING
MONEY AND HAPPINESS

ETHAN WILLIS
and RANDY GARN

BK

Berrett–Koehler Publishers, Inc.
San Francisco
a BK Life book

Berrett-Koehler Publishers, Inc.
235 Montgomery Street, Suite 650
San Francisco, CA 94104-2916
Tel: (415) 288-0260   Fax: (415) 362-2512   www.bkconnection.com

Ordering Information
Quantity sales. Special discounts are available on quantity purchases by corporations, associations, and others. For details, contact the "Special Sales Department" at the Berrett-Koehler address above.
Individual sales. Berrett-Koehler publications are available through most bookstores. They can also be ordered directly from Berrett-Koehler: Tel: (800) 929-2929; Fax: (802) 864-7626; www.bkconnection.com
Orders for college textbook/course adoption use. Please contact Berrett-Koehler: Tel: (800) 929-2929; Fax: (802) 864-7626.
Orders by U.S. trade bookstores and wholesalers. Please contact Ingram Publisher Services, Tel: (800) 509-4887; Fax: (800) 838-1149; E-mail: customer.service@ingrampublisherservices.com; or visit www.ingrampublisherservices.com/Ordering for details about electronic ordering.

Berrett-Koehler and the BK logo are registered trademarks of Berrett-Koehler Publishers, Inc.

Six Prosperity Practices and Polaris Point are trademarks of Prosper Holdings Inc.

Printed in the United States of America

Berrett-Koehler books are printed on long-lasting acid-free paper. When it is available, we choose paper that has been manufactured by environmentally responsible processes. These may include using trees grown in sustainable forests, incorporating recycled paper, minimizing chlorine in bleaching, or recycling the energy produced at the paper mill.

Library of Congress Cataloging-in-Publication Data
Willis, Ethan.
    Prosper : create the life you really want : six practices to find lasting money and happiness / Ethan Willis and Randy Garn.
        p. cm.
    Includes bibliographical references and index.
    ISBN 978-1-60994-070-6 (pbk. : alk. paper)
    1. Success in business.   2. Career development.   3. Success.   4. Happiness. I. Garn, Randy.   II. Title.
    HF5386.W564   2011
    650.1—dc23
                                                                                    2011025757

First Edition
16 15 14 13 12 11   10 9 8 7 6 5 4 3 2 1

Cover/Jacket designer: Leslie Waltzer/Crowfoot Design; Cover art: istockphoto.com/porocorex

For Devin Willis, my big brother,
whose courageous life
has been spent lifting others.

—ETHAN WILLIS

This book is dedicated to
James Nyle (Geedus) Garn,
my father, my hero.

—RANDY GARN

CONTENTS

PREFACE

With this book, we intend to do more than help you understand the nature of prosperity. We intend for you to become more prosperous.

There is a reason you are reading this book. There is some part of prosperity that you are seeking. It is our greatest desire to help you discover exactly what you are after.

Prosperity is a fundamental desire of all human beings. Most people pursue it, but some achieve it. Of those who do, fewer seem to sustain it. We believe that prosperity is something available for everyone who is willing to put forth the effort and make it happen, and as you read on, we will prove it to you.

We know that it is possible for people to have a life that balances the pursuit of prosperity with happiness. It's not easy, but it's not as hard as you may think it is. We have assisted thousands of people whose experiences and circumstances are similar to yours, who had the same desire as you to achieve long-lasting prosperity.

Some people did it by creating new businesses that allowed them to make money doing the things they are passionate about. Others worked within their companies to carve out lives of balance, meaning, and increased compensation. Some finally came to understand what they are really good at, then expanded their talents to create new careers. Still others learned new expertise, which made it possible to reinvent themselves in areas they had tremendous passion for.

WHO ARE WE TO TELL YOU ABOUT PROSPERITY?

We are two individuals who have devoted our lives to helping others create prosperity on their terms.

Since we founded Prosper in 1999, our company has coached over 75,000 people of all ages in eighty different countries to become more successful in their careers, establish businesses, and achieve long-term prosperity for themselves and their families. Helping people prosper (our company's mission statement) gives us our greatest sense of achievement.

With our combined backgrounds, we bring a unique perspective to the topic of prosperity, informed not only by our own success but by a deep desire to help people understand what prosperity really means to them and how to achieve it.

WHO WILL BENEFIT FROM READING THIS BOOK?

We wrote *Prosper* for people who are interested in creating a prosperity that will help them sustain and balance money and happiness. Everyone committed to improving some aspect of their lives will find value in these pages. When we wrote this book, we specifically thought of several categories of interests we wanted this book to serve. We hope you recognize yourself in one or more of these categories.

Personal Development. You realize that prosperity depends on you. You are ready to challenge some of the limiting beliefs, attitudes, or habits that have kept you from realizing your dreams, and you recognize that one-on-one coaching may be the answer. Have you discovered and tapped into your full potential? Are you firmly convinced that there is more to life than what you've already experienced? Are you looking to find more happiness, fulfillment, and success? You want to take control of your life, embrace the positive, and accomplish what's most important to you.

Career Development. You are currently employed and want to increase your value to the organization. You have made a significant investment in your current organization, and the organization has made a significant investment in you. You want to leverage that investment to recognize or create new opportunities for advancement and promotion.

Entrepreneurship. Your dream is to start and grow your own business in an area that you feel passionate about. Perhaps you are interested in making a living at doing what you love. Or maybe you have an idea for a new product and want to learn how to bring it to market. Passionate people have long embraced the entrepreneurial spirit. The most exciting business opportunities revolve around the power of the Internet, and you want to master such disciplines as social media, online auctions, search engine optimization, and Internet marketing.

Personal Finance and Investing. You have an interest in helping other people and yourself achieve their financial dreams, or you have a desire to effectively manage your personal finances and investments.

You want to make money work for you, save for a comfortable retirement, eliminate your debts, and build your own financial future. For those interested in specific areas of personal finance and investing, you may want to pursue prosperity opportunities in the stock market, real estate investing, or foreign exchange trading.

HOW TO PROSPER BY READING THIS BOOK

Simply put, we want you to prosper. To do that, there needs to be an agreement between the authors and the reader. A book can be a powerful instrument for change, and it starts with what you're doing right now. But reading, by itself, is unlikely to ensure sustainable prosperity. Prosperity is not achieved by reflection alone. We believe that if this book is to have meaningful impact on your pursuit of prosperity, you have to put what you learn into action. We don't want you to just read the book, mark it up, make notes in it, share it with someone you feel would benefit from it, and then read it again.

Prosper is an action guide to get you the life you really want. We wrote this book because we have created a process that has been the catalyst for many people just like you in achieving their dreams. This book offers proven strategies, tools, exercises, and insights that have helped thousands of people create prosperity—and we believe it can do the same for you.

Progress stems from reflection followed by profound action. That's why the conclusion of each chapter features a section we call "Prosperity Steps," where we offer exercises intended to help you understand the principles and then take action. All we ask of you is what we ask of our students: just give the steps a try. Each of them is based on actions that our students have reported to be useful. The more energy you invest in completing the Prosperity Steps at the end of each chapter, the more likely you are to benefit from our book.

You can find most of the Prosperity Steps, as well as some exercises that are not in the book, on our Web site at www.prosperbook .com. We are continually adding more prosperity resources online— we invite you to visit!

SIX PROSPERITY PRACTICES™

Think of someone you know who is prosperous. What is that person like? We bet there are certain habits or practices that this person abides by. In our research, we discovered Six Prosperity Practices that ignite the fire that is necessary to generate the commitment, energy, and courage to produce lasting prosperity. These practices are also, by necessity, a springboard to personal change through an understanding that prosperity is an internal journey—it requires from you the clarity to know what you really value and to have the courage to pursue it.

The Six Prosperity Practices flow from a careful study of thousands of our most successful coaching experiences, constituting over 5 million hours of coaching observation. At the same time, we were reaching out to a range of our most advanced students to evaluate how their prosperity looks now, years after they began working with us. What emerged from our survey astounded us. The Six Prosperity Practices predicted which students rose to the top and thrived in challenging environments. The students who followed these practices tended to be successful. In contrast, the outcomes for the students who had never quite mastered the practices tended to be unsatisfactory—or, even if they achieved a measure of success, it was fleeting.

The main section of this book devotes a chapter to each practice. In brief, the Six Prosperity Practices are:

Practice 1. Locate Your Polaris Point™. Everyone's Polaris Point is unique. It's your envisioned future: what you aspire to become, to achieve, to contribute, to create. It also includes the essential role money will play in those aspirations. A true Polaris Point is clear and compelling without being overly restrictive. It serves as a unifying focal point for your ongoing efforts, a goal that inspires creativity, and a catalyst for profound action.

Practice 2. Live in Your Prosperity Zone. When your earnings are aligned with your Polaris Point, we say you are living in the Prosperity Zone. There's no prosperity in having a Polaris Point that your earnings cannot support. At the same time, there's no prosperity if your earnings overwhelm your Polaris Point. You are living in your Prosperity Zone when your Polaris Point and earnings are in balance. This allows for sustainable prosperity.

Practice 3. Earn from Your Core. Sustainable prosperity flows from your unique talents and abilities. Make an inventory of what really motivates you. What do you do that feels more like play than work? The more you leverage the energy that flows from that kind of passion, the bigger the competitive advantage you can deliver, and the more satisfying the income will be. If you could be doing anything, what would it be? How can that be channeled into building prosperity?

Practice 4. Start with What You Already Have. You have "hidden" assets around you to waiting to be discovered. We show you how to find them and put them to use. The pursuit of prosperity is fueled by an awareness of the abundance you already have, not by the abundance you believe you lack. The fullness of your plate when you start, however little your plate contains, matters less than realizing that your plate isn't empty. Whether you start with a little or a lot, if you emphasize what you already have, you tend to end up with the most.

Practice 5. Commit to Your Prosperity Path. This is your new prosperous life that you have created—the road stands before you. You are now empowered by a clear direction that you know deep inside is directed to your personal Polaris Point. Apply your core abilities, resources, and life experiences, put metrics around it, and make yourself accountable. Something powerful happens when you *decide* to decide to live the life you really want.

Practice 6. Take Profound Action. Go for it! Implement the Prosperity Plan that marries personal satisfaction with a sustainable income stream. Persistence is required in taking this step and the next step on the long-distance path to prosperity. No get-rich-quick schemes, just the "law of the harvest."

A note about the word *student*. In this book, we frequently refer to the individuals who take part in our one-to-one education and coaching services as students. We use the term to refer to people of all ages and circumstances, past and present.

This book is not about incrementing your way to prosperity; it's about transformation—of your habits, attitudes, and responses. Our goal is to change your entire conception of what prosperity is, how to achieve it, and perhaps most of all, how to sustain it so that prosperity sustains you. Most people think that prosperity is like some distant, exotic land that, if you are very diligent or lucky, you can somehow visit for a moment. But if it's your goal to make yourself at home in the land of prosperity and put down some real roots—if you are, in short, determined to become prosperous—then read on.

YOUR PROSPERITY ASSESSMENT

HOW PROSPEROUS ARE YOU RIGHT NOW?

We're asking for a very specific reason. In this book, we make this promise: if you follow the practices we will describe, your level of prosperity will grow.

The Prosperity Assessment is a quick, insightful, multi-faceted evaluation, which is divided into three categories: money, happiness, and sustainability. It's easy and even fun to do online, and there's no charge to take it as many times as you want. The assessment should take about ten minutes. For each question, click the ranking that best describes your current situation. You will be asked to identify your perceived levels of prosperity in the three categories and compare them to your actual levels of prosperity. The assessment doesn't stop there however.

In an extended phase of the assessment you can invite your friends, co-workers, or family to take the assessment and answer the questions based on how they view your levels of prosperity. We've found that this type of "360-degree feedback" component helps identify areas that you overlooked, undervalued, or overvalued when you initially took the assessment on your own. We promise the results will be revealing.

Here is where you can find the Prosperity Assessment: www.prosperbook.com/assessment.

Go for it!

PERSONALIZED RESULTS

After you complete the Prosperity Assessment, you will receive a personalized report. In it, we identify various attributes of prosperity in which you are highly developed, developing, or need development. The report also generates a graph and accompanying materials that give you a comprehensive picture of your level of prosperity. A copy of your personalized report will be sent to you via e-mail so that you can study the results at your leisure. Please keep that report handy because we will ask you to refer to it later.

DISCOVER WHERE YOU ARE AND WHERE YOU NEED TO GO

Completing the Prosperity Assessment first will make your experience with this book significantly better. The most important part of your prosperity journey at this point is your attitude to a number of situations that we know predict a prosperous life. After you have taken inventory of your current prosperity strengths and weaknesses, we think the results we present will resonate in a different way. They will give you a significant advantage as you begin the path to greater prosperity. So go ahead—put down the book for a minute, and enter www.prosperbook.com/assessment in your Web browser. We think you will be glad you did.

Later, when you have finished this book and made the Six Prosperity Practices your own, we will invite you to take the Prosperity Assessment again. We predict there will be significant differences in your assessment. We believe that you will be even better positioned to leverage the lessons of this book in your prosperity journey.

INTRODUCTION

The Path to Prosperity
Isn't What You Think It Is

The journey to prosperity is like driving a car at night.
You can only see as far as the headlights, but you
make the whole trip that way.
—unknown

Much of what we are taught about prosperity and how we achieve it is just plain wrong.

Human beings have pursued prosperity since the dawn of civilization. Achingly few have achieved it. More recently, its pursuit has become an industry. There are thousands of books, courses, programs, and videos that promise to create prosperity. Yet for most of us, the path to prosperity seems bumpier than ever.

Today's financial turmoil has shaken everyone's conception of prosperity. Parents are concerned that their children will be unable to attain the same level of prosperity as they have. Everyone in this economy is facing challenges, whether it is college students starting their careers, middle managers trying to get ahead, entrpreneurs hoping to launch a business, or workers getting ready for retirement. All face harsh realities of employment, advancement, compensation, and job security.

WHAT IS PROSPERITY?

Now, before we go much farther, let's try to define what we're talking about. What exactly do we mean by *prosperity?*

The first question we ask our students is to define prosperity. Probably every one of our students has a unique definition of prosperity. That's as it should be since everyone has a different definition of what a prosperous life would mean for them.

Here's just a sampling of how people we have surveyed around the world defined prosperity.

Lisa *Prosperity is a way of living and thinking, and not just having money or things.*

Deepak *Prosperity means having the time and financial freedom to enjoy life at your own leisure.*

Javier *Being in the flow, having what you need at the time you need it.*

Pearl *The ability to achieve personal growth and financial security without sacrificing family and health.*

Dieter *Not living paycheck to paycheck. Not having to worry about money for bills.*

Monique *Prosperity is a blend of health, wealth, familial fulfillment, and personal self satisfaction, blended correctly and in balance and harmony.*

Tom *To be able to do what I want, when I want.*

Maria *Prosperity includes making the best of what you have, accepting the physical conditions that you can't change while working toward good health, giving of yourself to family and friends, working with our community to help those in need, being true to your religion, with enough finances to live comfortably.*

Larry *Being debt free with the ability to pay cash for everything and to have cash available for emergency situations.*

Jann *Living a rich life, one of love and compassion, wealth and complete joy, one of caring and sharing, filled with laughter and exploration; the joy of loving a child; seeing the world and its wonders—to be able to do this in life is prosperity.*

Pat *The ability to weather all storms of life—financial or physical—and to assist friends to cope with their struggles by financially coming alongside them and helping them rise above the tumult.*

We noticed many commonalities. Many of the definitions included terms such as money, wealth, income, security, savings, health, family, and friends. We were struck by how many of the definitions of prosperity included the word *love*. It was also heartening to see how many definitions included service to others, volunteering, serving the community, and other selfless acts.

Now It's Your Turn

Here's your chance to come up with a working definition of prosperity, one that works uniquely for you.

Go ahead, you try it. What does prosperity mean to you? Take a minute to think about it. Write down a sentence or two. We'll wait. And please don't worry about pinning yourself down. We're not going to hold you to what you come up with now. Later in the book, you will have a chance to revisit the question. It should be interesting to see how your perspective on prosperity shifts after you have read this book.

PROSPERITY DEFINED

We see prosperity as multidimensional. When you are happy, when you have enough money and are at peace with how you are earning that money, this leads to the sustainable state that we describe as *prosperity*. Balancing these three things—money, happiness, plus sustainability—leads to prosperity. The prosperity that we value depends on creating income consistent with our inner selves, our core selves; without that, no amount of external compensation can fully make us happy.

Our definition is represented by the following equation:

MONEY + HAPPINESS + SUSTAINABILITY = PROSPERITY

These are terms with lots of meanings. Let us tell you what we mean by money, happiness, and sustainability in the context of prosperity.

Money

Money is important, no doubt about it. We subscribe to the notion that while money isn't everything, it is an indispensable component of prosperity. Money is not, as has been asserted, the root of all evil. It is the want of money that is the problem, and by "want" we are talking of both the desperation for and the constant unfilled need for money. The lesson of history is that it's the love of money above what we truly value that creates misery.

Money is a key concept of this book. If it wasn't, then it might as well just be another book about happiness. This book is not about happiness—it is about how money interacts with our lives and how we spend our days and efforts earning it. This book is less about a means to an end and more about the means and whether your true potential and passions are being fully engaged in the process. Once they are, we are convinced that more money will come and you will be able to sustain your efforts and be happiest.

By money, we mean income sufficient to support your goals. Earning enough money is absolutely essential to our concept of prosperity. Earning money is the difference between a business and a hobby. We believe it is possible to be happy with a hobby, but it takes income to generate and sustain prosperity.

The big question, of course, is, How much money is enough to ensure sustainable prosperity? The answer: Enough to support your financial dreams in a way that honors your deeply held values and principles, but not so much that your money distracts or alienates you from those very values and principles. The trick is to make your work feel more like an activity you enjoy than an activity you dread.

Happiness

For the purposes of this book, we are including under the general concept of happiness the following elements:

- State of mind—having positive feelings about ourselves and the world
- Authenticity—living life consistent with our deepest beliefs, values, and principles, and knowing that our earnings are aligned with our passions and purpose
- Commitment—adhering to what we most value, such as family and relationships
- Health and wellness—pursuing a prosperity that supports complete health in mind and body

It is beyond the scope of this book to summarize all that has been written about happiness. Here's how it looks to us. When we jump out of bed ready to live the day as full and completely as we can, when we make money doing what we enjoy, when we are living a life consistent with our beliefs, when we are satisfied with our relationships, when we are in touch with our health, when we are moving forward to realize our dreams, that's happiness.

Sustainability

We believe that sustainability is the third and most overlooked component of prosperity. The concept of sustainability in the context of wealth is elastic and in flux, but we think that if you can answer "yes" to these four questions, the prosperity you seek is more likely sustainable than not.

1. **Can I feel good about it?** People rightly get anxious when the money they make comes from doing something outside their comfort zone. Sustainable prosperity comes when we align our earnings with what motivates us and gives our lives meaning. When we love the work we do because we care about it, we become more attentive to detail, more committed to excellence, and more productive. After all, if you love what you're doing, it's not work. More importantly, working from your core shields you from being defeated by the occasional setback or failure.

2. **Can I sustain the work required over the long term?** Basically, do you have the passion and interest to keep at it for years and decades? Burning out or destroying your health by doing something that saddles you down is not a long-term solution, and any prosperity you generate using such approaches eventually evaporates. If you wake up each day in dread of going to work, in the long run you won't be good at your job, and you

won't be as successful. Someone who is passionate about the work will likely outperform you.

3. **Is the prosperity I contemplate ethical, beneficial to others, and environmentally sound?** Success can no longer be measured by economic profit alone. You also need to ask whether it is ethical, moral, and of value to others. Is your ethical compass pointing true north? Only wealth that meets the needs of the present without compromising the ability of future generations to meet their own needs is sustainable wealth.

4. **Does it offer lasting value?** There's no room in sustainable prosperity for get-rich-quick schemes or flash-in-the-pan opportunities. Sustainable prosperity is based on the law of the harvest, the deliberate concentration of the life you want. And not just for you, but also for the communities in which you work and live.

PROSPER FROM THE INSIDE OUT

Most people think of prosperity as an external event, something outside their control, something that happens to you, like an inheritance or winning a lottery.

Is that the way you think about prosperity? In such an externally driven state of identity, life seems uncertain and fragile. Everything that happens to us defines who we are. We become our circumstances. The more we envision prosperity as something that exists "out there," as something to be dominated, the less likely it will satisfy us. It will be as if we wrestled a fine suit of clothes to the ground only to find that it just doesn't fit very well.

We have a neighbor who just came back from a whirlwind vacation. He visited ten European countries in as many days. "I did Italy in one day," he boasted. We agree that he "did" Italy, but what did Italy do to him? How was he changed? Was his perspective altered in any way? What does he have to show for his collision with a different language and culture? He may have happened on Italy, but did Italy in any meaningful sense happen on him? Our neighbor is satisfied with his vacation, and we have no wish to criticize him. But for us, prosperity is a pursuit—not just a stop along your path through life. This book is designed to help you achieve the kind of prosperity that's sustainable over a lifetime.

NOT ALL POLARIS POINTS ARE HONORED

People who ignore their Polaris Point do so at peril of their health, happiness, and prosperity. A good example of this is a very talented songwriter we'll call Jessica. She not only has a passion for song writing but has a real aptitude for it. One of her first songs was selected and recorded by a leading country artist. Jessica received over $1,000 for that song, plus royalties, and she says it was the sweetest money she has ever earned. We think that she has more than enough natural talent to compete with the best songwriters in Nashville and make a decent living doing what she loves.

But to pursue her Polaris Point, Jessica would have to take a leap and quit her job.

Jessica is not yet ready to do that. She is currently working at an insurance company, in a secure job with a salary of about $35,000 per year. She has health insurance, paid holidays, and other benefits. The job meets her financial needs—but those are the only needs it meets. Jessica is miserable chained to a desk. All she wants to do is write songs, mingle with musicians, and be part of the Nashville professional music scene. She fantasizes about writing a hit song, and then she goes back to the task at hand. She realizes that the gap between what she most wants and what she is willing to settle for is eating her up. Jessica regrets every day she fails to follow her Polaris Point, but so far she has not acted.

THE PROSPERITY JOURNEY STARTS WITH QUESTIONS

These are just some of the questions this book asks you to consider. You can answer these questions by yourself, but some people find it easier to do with a partner. Make sure to write your answers down.

1. What does my ideal lifestyle look like?
2. How much money do I need to maintain my ideal lifestyle?
3. What can I do to improve the most important relationships in my life?
4. How important is a sense of physical well-being?
5. How much exercise do I need each week?
6. What can I do to improve myself?
7. What can I do to improve my self-image and self-confidence?
8. How do I see my spiritual relationship to prosperity?
9. What makes me happiest? Why?
10. How much do I value an environmentally sustainable life?

We listen very carefully to what our students say about what they value. But sometimes we can't hear what our students are telling us because their actions are so loud. In the most extreme cases, we sometimes say, "Don't tell us what you value. Show us your credit card statement, and *we'll* tell you what you value."

DOES MONEY MAKE YOU HAPPIER?

Perhaps the central belief most common to our students is that high income is directly associated with happiness. It seems to them that the more money they have, the happier and more satisfied they will be. We've learned that it does little good to challenge this belief even though we know it is not always the rule.

The most certain thing we can say about wealth and happiness is that money does indeed make one happier, but only to the extent that people can meet their basic needs such as food and housing. In other words, if a person is in poverty—lacking enough food to eat, decent housing, and transportation—and feels unhappy about it, then certainly money will contribute to happiness. When happiness is related to basic human needs, there's nothing better than money to ensure happiness.

But that relationship quickly breaks down when one's basic needs are satisfied. After that, measured happiness levels change very little as incomes grow over time.

MORE THAN MONEY

Prosperity is always about a determination to change one's situation, and almost always that determination has something to do with money. We respect this relationship. Determination and money certainly go together. We think the pursuit of money is commendable and respectable. It is one's intentions that need the greater inspection.

At the same time, prosperity is about more than just financial success. Of those who actually achieve financial success, we have seen that the victory is often short-lived, inconsistent, or anticlimactic. At the same time, we have coached some people to create lives of breathtaking wealth, balance, and, yes, grace. We call this sustainable prosperity.

The following story illustrates the power of how people see the world in a different light when they are in touch with their true values.

In the wake of a terrible hurricane that did a lot of damage to coastal communities in North Carolina, a beach geologist was being interviewed. The reporter asked him what hurricanes do to beaches. Now, most people know the answer to that question. Hurricanes are very destructive. Beaches are torn up, and residents get very upset. At one point during the interview, the geologist said, "You know, I can't wait to get out on those beaches again as soon as this storm has passed."

"What do you expect to find out there?" the interviewer asked.

Before reading further, how would you answer the question? After a destructive hurricane, what would you look for?

Here's what the geologist said: "I expect to find a new beach."

What would it mean if we looked at change as that beach geologist does, where we look beyond our current way of thinking? Where we could celebrate the newness that was just revealed rather than grieve for what was lost? The story reminds us that too often we are surprised by change in a way that makes it impossible for us to welcome it. We actually see newness as a stumbling block to our plans.

We invite you to equate reading this book as a fresh look at a brand new beach in your life. Look at it as a brand new view of how money and happiness are balanced in your life.

JOIN US FOR THE PROSPERITY JOURNEY

The best way to determine your definition of prosperity is to be crystal clear in your own mind about what a life of prosperity looks like for you. The more detailed you can be about your circumstances, desires, and goals, the closer your definition will be. This is not just an academic exercise. Based on watching thousands of students working to realize their visions of prosperity, we can tell you that the more clearly you can articulate what exactly prosperity means to you, the more likely it is that you will achieve it.

To each reader, we want you to know it is our life's work to help you *Prosper*. We look forward to being your guides on your journey to prosperity. We invite you to define it, create it, and live it!

CHAPTER 1

LOCATE YOUR POLARIS POINT

The Master in the art of living makes little distinction
between his work and his play, his labor and his
leisure, his mind and his body, his education and his
recreation, his love and his religion.

He hardly knows which is which. He simply pursues
his vision of excellence in whatever he does, leaving
others to decide whether he is working or playing.
To him, he is always doing both.

—*from the Buddhist tradition*

By your Polaris Point, we mean the ultimate destination that guides you, that inspires you when you're making progress, and that rights you when you get off course. It's the sparkle that lights your way in the dark.

In astronomy, there is but one Polaris, otherwise known as the North Star. Among the billions of stars, it is unique in that it is the beacon most nearly aligned to the north spin axis of the Earth. As the Earth turns, stars and constellations move through the sky—but not Polaris. It stays fixed in the sky relative to Earth, and any time it can be seen, true north is revealed. The result has guided travelers since the dawn of human history.

Polaris, the North Star, has ensured the fortunes of countless navigators on land and sea, and the concept of the Polaris Point can help guide you. All it requires is that you carefully choose a spot on the horizon, making sure to steadily move toward it. This is your Polaris Point. For the time being, think of it as defining the only direction worth following.

In this chapter, we will help you locate your Polaris Point.

YOUR UNIQUE POLARIS POINT

Everyone's Polaris Point is unique. It's the envisioned future of what you aspire to become, to achieve, to contribute, to create and how all of that relates to money. A true Polaris Point is clear and compelling without being overly restrictive. It serves as a unifying focal point for your ongoing earning efforts, a goal that inspires creativity, and a catalyst for profound action (see Chapter 6).

Here's the way we think about the Polaris Points. Imagine that you are at the end of a well-lived life in which you have met all the goals you have set for yourself. You have no regrets. You are invited to your own funeral. Now, what is it that you hope people will say about your life? If you've aligned your life with your authentic self, chances are many of the eulogies will mention your Polaris Point— not because they heard you talk about it, but because your actions and contributions spoke convincingly to them.

WHERE'S THE MONEY?

A Polaris Point is unique in that it always addresses your relation-ship with money. Yes, it usually also talks about your ethics, values, and passions. It can reflect your hopes and desires for happiness and prosperity. But it always defines a fundamental aspect of how important money is to you. Whatever amount of money you believe you will require, your Polaris Point has something to say about how your sense of prosperity determines the income you intend to generate.

Let us show you what we mean. We asked five people to share their Polaris Points.

Ellen *Teaching is my joy and passion. Seeing the transformation in young people's lives is what I want to spend my health, wealth, and self doing for the rest of my life. Instead of filling bank accounts, I want to fill the minds of future leaders with knowledge and integrity. I want to do this side by side with my husband.*

Floyd *I want to provide for members of my family and extended family who do not have the means to achieve their own dreams and aspirations. I am okay working sixty hours a week as long as it provides for their aspirations and I can maintain healthy strong relationships with them. Money is less important to me than a lasting legacy.*

Hector *I want to leave a legacy of honor, service, and excellence for posterity. I am dedicated to a lifetime of defending my country as a member of the armed forces. I know I will not make as much as I could in other professions; however, a pattern of honor and safety for my children is more valuable than gold.*

Steven *I desire to live my life to the fullest. Money is best invested in experiences. I want to create a life that is a string of exceptional life experiences. In order to do this, I need to create substantial income that allows me to have flexibility. I will work hard, but I will also play hard. I will not let the pursuit of money overtake my goal "to seize the day."*

Tamara *I want a life that is simple and worry-free. I want to put down roots in a neighborhood and live there for a long time. I want to only work twenty to thirty hours a week and enjoy the time with my children,* friends, and pets. These relationships will come before the pursuit of material things, not the things I need. I am willing to spend much less and live in a smaller house in order to do this. I will control money, and it will not control my quality of life.

THE AUTHORS' POLARIS POINTS

For most people, determining their own Polaris Point and putting it into concrete language can be one of the most challenging tasks they will ever face. We ourselves struggled with the process of identifying our Polaris Points, and we think it might be helpful if we showed you a bit of how we arrived at them, a bit about the circumstances from which they originated, and how we express them.

Ethan Willis *Before I give you my own Polaris Point, I'd like you to know a little bit about me. While growing up in Southern California, I cannot remember a house that my family ever owned. My six brothers and sisters shared everything. What I remember most is that, while there was not much to share, we all got along, and we were happy sharing. It wasn't until much later that I realized how little we actually had. Still, it often seemed to me that our family enjoyed some seasons of prosperity.*

My mother worked as a night shift nurse helping deliver high-risk babies. She taught me that I could be anything in life if I just found the right solution and applied it. My father was born on a dairy farm and taught me the value of getting up early and working hard. He would leave the house at 5:00 a.m. to work at two different hospitals as a respitory specialist, and not come home until late. But however tired he was, my father would wake all the children at 4:30 a.m. for family prayer before he left. We read scriptures and expressed gratitude for the blessings of life.

My father's goal in life was to provide for his children a better life than he himself had. In this goal, my father was clear that a better life meant more than just money. He spoke about the importance of being happy

20

and living purposefully. I was a teenager when my father died of cancer. To honor his sacrifice, I committed to deliver on the goal that he set on behalf of his children. My conscious path to prosperity began at that moment.

I first sought God's presence. I wanted to understand what this life was really about, where my father went, and what I could do to ensure I could be with him again. After passing up such opportunities as playing baseball for a Los Angeles Dodgers scout team, I decided to go to Brazil on a volunteer service mission. During my time in one of the poorest parts of Brazil, I learned something about poverty and prosperity.

When I looked closer, I saw something totally unexpected. People in the exact same circumstances with the same levels of income experienced their situations in completely different ways. Some families dwelled in abject poverty. But others, with no more resources to their names, lived lives that looked much more satisfying, even prosperous. I was fascinated by the clear implications that, on some level, poverty and prosperity are states of mind.

When I returned to the United States after two years, I knew two things: (1) prosperity is a choice, and (2) only you can define how much money you need to be prosperous. I set a goal to earn enough money and do it in a way that helped others do the same. That was the beginning of my Polaris Point. Since then, I have pursued prosperity in many ways: from feeling trapped by my job, moving up the corporate ladder; to bootstrapping my business, scraping to make payroll each week; to selling pest control services door to door, raising five children, balancing family relationships and the demands of the world; to working with famous authors and millionaires, experiencing Harvard Business School's perspectives of prosperity, seeing people in eighty countries strive for prosperity, employing over 2,000 people, and struggling to find balance between money and happiness and purpose.

My last fifteen years have been spent trying to define, live, and teach prosperity. We all have a story, and I hope sharing a little of mine can help you understand how I might be able to help you on your path.

ETHAN'S POLARIS POINT

I will put off instant gratification for long-term prosperity. I will treat my time as an asset. I will invest the greater amounts in the things that will last longest. My greatest priorities are my wife, children, extended family, dear friends, and commitments to the Divine. Earning will be to support my family and to build people, businesses, and ideas that will better the world. The earnings of profits will be the applause customers give me because of the value they receive.

Randy Garn *I grew up in a small town with parents who taught me the value of integrity and hard work. My father and mother both taught at the local high school. My mother was the English teacher and debate coach. My father was the athletic director and the head football coach of the high school football team.*

One of the central learning experiences of my life was watching my father coach and inspire student athletes to reach their full potential, and not always just in football. His example cemented in me the power of teamwork and the importance of a good coach. From my father, I learned that if I wanted something and worked hard for it, then nothing was impossible. I learned that money was important, but many other things were more so. To me, the great sources of well-being and happiness are the relationships that I nourish and which nourish me.

I have always tried to live each day to the fullest and have a cheerful, positive outlook in every circumstance. I have only one life to live and only one opportunity to leave my mark on this world. I want to take that opportunity and leave the world in better shape than I found it. In my view, the very best way to do this is by helping as many other people as I can and looking for the best in other people rather than the flaws. To lift another person, you have to be standing on higher ground.

I have a great passion for innovation and entrepreneurship. I love helping other businesspeople grow and flourish. I am especially proud of my role in helping start several businesses and steward them to success, jobs, profits, and value for others to enjoy. Having enough money is important, but my passion is helping people take an idea and transform it into a thriving business.

RANDY'S POLARIS POINT

I found my Polaris Point when I came to understand that through technology, education, and hard work, I can help change the world one person at a time. I love being a coach, a guide, a positive motivating force in another's life. I cherish human relationships. I have a unique ability to connect people together in a way that creates lasting value. Money is important to me, but my passion is being the connection between what others desire to become and how to get there. I truly love to see others succeed.

POLARIS POINTS IN ACTION

In his book *The Transparent Leader*, Herb Baum, the former chairman and CEO of Dial, illustrates how Polaris Points operate by working to keep people aligned with their highest aspirations. There is intense competition between his company and Colgate in such areas as soap, shampoo, and other billion-dollar market segments. He recounts receiving a telephone call from Reuben Mark, the chairman and CEO of Colgate-Palmolive:

> I have a lot of respect for the company [Colgate], and I knew Reuben to be an outstanding CEO with an excellent reputation. The day he called, he said that he had in his possession a CD containing Dial Soap's marketing plan for the year. It had been given to him by a member of his sales force (a former Dial employee who had taken it with him when he left to join Colgate), and it meant that one of Dial's most important product line's strategies had been revealed, and could result in the loss of revenue, profits, and market share.
>
> "Herb," Reuben said, "one of our new salespeople gave this CD to one of my sales managers. I'm not going to look at this information,

and I'm sending it back to you right now. I'll handle it on this end." It was the clearest case of leading with honor and transparency I've witnessed in my career. After all, who expects a CEO to call his competitor and tell him they have a copy of their detailed business strategy? If he hadn't, I never would have known, but that one call gave me more insight into his character than anything else.

It wasn't hard to see why he had been so successful in his career. He knew he didn't need to gain an unfair competitive advantage to succeed, even when he was presented with the opportunity. He chose not to abandon his leadership style, and he had the courage to stick to his principles even when it meant giving up confidential information that could have helped his company gain an edge. (Baum and Kling 2004, 31)

To us, what Baum called leading with honor and transparency actually describes the Colgate CEO's Polaris Point. We'd guess that early in his career Reuben Mark decided that the only legitimate success was success that he earned and that he would not tolerate nor take unfair advantage in any form. The honor and transparency that Baum described are very real because they are consequences of Mark's Polaris Point. Everyone can be tempted to violate what one knows to be right. Being clear about how he would or would not make money guided his business decision. When temptation strikes, it's very important to have solid Polaris Point values to guide you.

POLARIS POINT MENTORS

Some people instinctively know what their Polaris Point is. But most people, like us, have to work at it.

One great way to get a clearer view of what your Polaris Point might be is to think about the people you most admire. We think of these people as Polaris Point Mentors. They can be people you know, such as your parents or a beloved teacher. They can be world leaders, famous scientists, athletes, astronauts, or other celebrities that you view from afar. The odds are that if you feel this person's life represents something you yearn to emulate, there is an element of your Polaris Point in that person's experience.

Clayton Christensen, an influential professor at the Harvard Business School, is an individual who is absolutely committed to a Polaris Point that, to us, is about the integrity of never compromising over the things that matter most (Christensen 2010).

Most of us know the difference between right and wrong, but sometimes it's tempting to loosen our standards. We whisper to ourselves, "Okay, I know that as a general rule I shouldn't be doing this. But in this particular extenuating circumstance, just for me, just this once, it's not so bad. I'll never do it again." Sound familiar? Many of us go through these rationalizations. This often happens with the choices we make in how we go about making a living.

The technical term for this moral wiggling, Professor Christensen taught us, is the *marginal cost*. The marginal cost of doing something wrong "just this once" always seems alluringly low. It suckers you in, and you don't ever look at where that path ultimately is headed. This compromises your Polaris Point.

PICK YOUR POLARIS POINT
OR ELSE IT WILL PICK YOU

When it comes to deciding on what your Polaris Point should be, just make sure your aim is true. That's why starting with what you already have and working from your core are so critical.

In the movie *Up in the Air*, Ryan Bingham (played by George Clooney) has a Polaris Point that consists of collecting 10 million frequent flier miles. Bingham believes that when he finally gets all those miles, he will be happy. He fantasizes about the perks and status that will result: the front-of-the-line access, premium seats, lavish attention, free wine, and, most of all, being recognized by name. Status, even more than money, can be a powerful motivator. When Bingham finally hits his 10-million-mile goal during a flight from Chicago to Omaha, the chief pilot of American Airlines makes it a big deal while presenting the coveted graphite card that allows him to access his own private customer service representative. But the satisfaction is short-lived. Bingham's interest in this goal was already waning—he'd already started looking elsewhere for fulfillment—and that's why this moment was so sad.

Happiness theory suggests that personal priorities are very important in determining one's satisfaction. For example, people who emphasize generosity and selflessness and feel good about giving away a part of their prosperity tend to be happier than those who focus on obtaining more and more material goods. In the film, Ryan Bingham experiences this phenomenon. Although now he can book first-class vacations to exotic locations anywhere in the world without cost, he has little interest in getting on another airplane. But he gets satisfaction from transferring some miles from his account so his sister can finally fulfill a life-long dream to visit Paris.

If you find that you're being evasive about your Polaris Point, chances are that something is out of alignment and your path is likely not sustainable. We see this evasiveness played out in *Up in the Air* when Ryan Bingham talks to Natalie, a young woman he is mentoring.

NATALIE: Okay, you gotta fill me in on the miles thing. What is that about?

RYAN: I don't spend a nickel if I can help it unless it somehow profits my mileage account.

NATALIE: So what are you saving up for? Hawaii, South of France?

RYAN: It's not like that. The miles are the goal.

NATALIE: That's it? You're saving just to save?

RYAN: Just say I have a number in mind and I haven't hit it yet.

NATALIE: That's a little abstract. What's the target?

RYAN: I'd rather not [say].

NATALIE: Is it a secret target?

We recommend going public with your Polaris Point for a number of reasons. First, if you can be open about your destination, it's a good sign you're on a path that's sustainable. Transparency is good. Second, being visible with your destination allows others to accompany you or even assist you.

THE ONLY DIRECTION IS NORTH

The one direction in the pursuit of prosperity is the bearing indicated by your Polaris Point. Whenever you are unsure if you are on the right path, all you have to do is locate the Polaris Point. Keep your eyes on your own personal Polaris Point, and you will always be moving in the right direction.

As you tack toward your Polaris Point, you will find yourself off course from time to time. This is normal. The important thing is that you notice when you are off the path and make small corrections.

27

It turns out that without a reference point, people literally walk in circles. New research from the Max Planck Institute for Biological Cybernetics in Tübingen, Germany, found that without a reference point, people just can't walk in a straight line (Souman et al. 2009). Using GPS devices, researchers studied participants who walked for several hours in the Sahara desert in Tunisia and in the Bienwald forest in Germany. The results showed that participants were able to walk in a straight path only when they could see the sun or moon; as soon as reference points disappeared behind clouds, participants started walking in circles without even knowing it. No exceptions.

That's why it's absolutely necessary for you to have your Polaris Point in mind at all times. Without it, you may think you're making a straight line toward prosperity, but it's probably an illusion, and in reality your progress is at best very inefficient or at worst going no-where fast. Everyone needs a reference point.

LOCATE YOUR POLARIS POINT

Prosperity Steps

This exercise will guide you through the process of identifying your Polaris Point and framing a statement that describes it in actionable terms. The process starts by clarifying your values and their relationship to money. After you go through the first three steps, you will be ready to frame a Polaris Point informed by your most deeply held values.

Complete this Prosperity Step online at www.prosperbook.com/PS1.

What You Value Most

Identify your important work and personal values. Make a list of things you want most in life. Upon completion choose the top ten.

Elimination

Now that you have identified the top ten things, eliminate seven more until you are left with your top three most important things. They are likely to be the basis of your Polaris Point.

Evaluation

With respect to the top three remaining on your list, consider the following questions.

1. What do your selections have in common?
2. Does the way you earn your income today align with the things most important to you?
3. What does the list say about what you are expecting from yourself?

4. How would your life and career be different if you consistently focused on those things you value most?

5. Does this list reflect the way you actually conduct your life?

Define Your Polaris Point

Write out an identifying statement that embraces the three things you deeply value most. Start the sentence with "My Polaris Point includes . . ."

Next, write out a framing statement of your Polaris Point, embracing those three selections.

Example

Suppose the three selections were meaningful career, enough money to retire at sixty years old, and a deeper relationship with Terry.

The identifying response

My Polaris Point includes a meaningful career, enough money to retire at sixty years old, and a deeper relationship with Terry.

The framing response

I promise to guide every aspect of my life by my commitment to a meaningful career and focusing on my retirement plan in order to retire at sixty, while continuing to build a deeper relationship with Terry.

Now, there are millions of ways to express a commitment to any set of priorities. In fact, there are probably as many Polaris Point statements as there are people in the world. We can't put words in your mouth—only you can do that. We know it's not easy: defining your Polaris Point requires real self-interrogation followed by sustained reflection of what matters most. It often feels like the hardest work in the world.

CHAPTER 2

LIVE IN YOUR PROSPERITY ZONE

*My goal wasn't to make a ton of money. It was to
build good computers.*

—Steve Wozniak, co-founder of Apple

As an exercise, a group of individuals were asked to make a list of the "Seven Wonders of Your World." Most people are familiar with the Seven Wonders of the Ancient World (the pyramids, the Hanging Gardens of Babylon, the light house at Alexandria, etc.), most of which no longer exist.

The individuals took a few minutes to write down their lists and, one by one, they shared what they regarded as the most miraculous examples of wonder on Earth. Although there were some differences in the lists, many of the responses mentioned some combination of the following natural and man-made wonders:

The Grand Canyon

The Golden Gate Bridge

The Great Wall of China

Mount Everest

The Taj Mahal

The Panama Canal

The Empire State Building

St. Peter's Basilica

The Hubble Space Telescope

One individual (let's call her Ruth) still hadn't finished her list. When asked if she was having trouble, Ruth replied, "Yes a little, I can't quite make up my mind because there are so many to choose from." The facilitator responded, "Well, tell us what you have so far." Ruth hesitated and then looked down at her list. "I think the seven wonders of the modern world are…"

To see

To hear

To touch

To smell

To laugh

To feel

To love

The room grew silent with the realization that Ruth was onto something profound. Every item on her list was not only free but freely available without limit to everyone in the room.

In this story, Ruth gently reminded the group, and no less the facilitators, that no amount of money can buy the most precious and wondrous things in life. These are the properties of our life that we overlook and precisely the lesson that this story profoundly illustrates.

What we want our students to do is to notice the wonders that do actually exist, the ones they can visit and touch, whether it's a remote destination or right next door. This thought exercise is very much in keeping with the Six Prosperity Practices that we cover in this book, and it is part of a values clarification exercise that we have conducted dozens of times.

WELCOME TO THE PROSPERITY ZONE

The Prosperity Zone is when you are able to find your area of balance with money, happiness, and sustainability. In other words, you are in the Prosperity Zone when you are living your best life, when what makes you money makes you and other people happy, when work doesn't seem like work at all, and when you enjoy every waking moment. Your Prosperity Zone is the place where what you love to do more than anything in the whole world also makes you money. You stay in your Prosperity Zone by working from your core and doing what you love.

It's true that at times more money predicts more happiness. But the relationship is actually a little more complicated. We gain little in the way of prosperity if our expenses increase to the same extent our income does. In such cases, our standard of living may increase, but living hand to mouth does little to promote happiness. True Prosperity grows not just as your happiness or income increases, but as a function of the difference between happiness and income.

How do you create sustainable prosperity? Just make sure that the difference between what you earn and what you need to fund your Polaris Point is not only positive but growing over time.

The Hedonic Treadmill

Have you ever wanted something really bad and worked hard for it, thinking that once you had it you'd be satisfied—only to find that, when you actually obtained it, you were satisfied for a while but then you noticed it wasn't quite enough and you set your sights on something else? This is a normal human tendency with a fancy name. Researchers call this the *hedonic treadmill* (Brickman, Coates, and Janoff-Bulman). Also known as hedonic adaptation, this is the tendency to quickly return to your previous level of happiness despite acquiring things you had previously thought would make you much happier.

We've seen this over and over again. Many of our students actually achieve a period of having both happiness and enough money. But then it falls apart for some of them. The pattern is all too familiar. As income starts to increase, happiness picks up, which leads to a time of prosperity. The problem is that, for some of our students, the resulting sense of prosperity is short-lived. Happiness begins to fade as they get used to their increased income, their appetites grow, and they lose control of their expenses. They get caught in a pattern of dissatisfaction, which leads to even more spending.

Don't get us wrong. We think it's great for our newly wealthy students to spend what they have earned. But it is essential to keep the spending in support of your Polaris Point. That's why keeping your eye on sustainability is so important—it protects the prosperity you are working so hard to create.

The Lawyer and the Janitor

Consider two men. One became a very successful corporate lawyer, and the other became a janitor in a public high school. Both men want basically the same things out of life: financial security, quality time with their children and spouses, and a measure of happiness and autonomy to pursue their hobbies and contribute to the community.

The lawyer makes $750,000 a year, has a beautiful home at a prestigious address in town, drives a luxury car, and has the respect of his colleagues in the legal system. From the outside, it appears that the lawyer is living a prosperous life. But a closer look reveals a more complicated reality. The lawyer is stressed because, although he is making a high six-figure income, he has to work seventy hours a week to pay the mortgage and is still living paycheck to paycheck. His children are growing up without him, his work has crowded his hobbies out of his life, and contributing to the community is just another item on his "to do" list, which seems to get ever longer. He has lost sight of his Polaris Point.

Meanwhile, let's look at the janitor. His income is a fraction of the lawyer's income. Although he may not see big raises, he enjoys fixing things and is good at his work, so his position is secure. His shift is 4:00 AM to 12:00 noon, so he is home to spend afternoons with his children, helping them with their homework and preparing family dinners. His residence is modest, but soon it will be paid off. The family has discretionary income for field trips and boy scout camp, and he can afford weekend getaways with his wife. He volunteers at a senior center and enjoys his hobby of refurbishing vintage cars. His income is more than sufficient to fund the lifestyle he has chosen, and his savings grow every month.

Prosperity comes from knowing what your individual core talents and passions are, happily creating a profitable activity around those talents and passions, and implementing that activity as an income plan that is sustainable over the long term. When you have these elements in balance, we say you are in the Prosperity Zone.

Income and Happiness

We have spent over ten years watching our students navigate the relationship between income and happiness. It's clear that income increases student happiness when it allows them to live a middle-class life, but it does little or nothing to increase happiness thereafter. Yes, students who earn $100,000 per year tend to be happier than those who earn $25,000 per year. But students who earn $1 million per year are not always ten times happier than those who earn $100,000. What happens is that as students make more money, they simply reset the happiness bar. If they make $50,000 and don't seem much happier, they decide that they will surely be happy when they make $75,000.

The reality is that however much some students may earn, many of them never quite find the happiness they seek by focusing on income alone.

The role of money and happiness is not at all straightforward. Let us show you what we mean. Consider two options in which you earn different amounts of money. Which would you choose?

- An annual income of $50,000 when the average income is $25,000 per year.
- An annual income of $75,000 when the average income is $100,000 per year.

If you assume people make rational decisions that are in their best interests, you would conclude that most people would choose the second option. After all, it puts an extra $25,000 per year into their pockets. But, in fact, up to half the people presented with these scenarios select the lower income option (Shermer 2008). The science of behavioral economics comes to the rescue to explain why. It seems that the absolute amount of money we make is less important than how our income compares with others'. Many of us would rather settle for less as long as we get bragging rights for earning above the average. Status, it turns out, is a great motivator.

So if money, by itself, is not guaranteed to bring happiness, what does? According to Glenn Firebaugh and Laura Tach of Harvard University, the following factors are the best predictors of happiness: physical health, income, education, and marital status—and in that order. Income is only the second best predictor of happiness. For most people, health is first.

A Simple Money Quiz

Take this simple quiz, and see how it applies to you. Fill in the following two statements with a specific number.

1. My current annual income is:
2. In order to accomplish my Polaris Point, my annual income would need to be:

What multiple of your current salary will it take for you to have financial security? We have given this test to all of our coaching students. Most indicated that their annual income would need to be about twice what they currently were earning for them to feel free from money worries. Students who made $20,000 a year believed it would take roughly $40,000 a year in order to be financially content; students who made $100,000 said they would need to earn about $200,000.

A funny thing happens when students actually see their incomes double. In general, the financial security and happiness that they anticipated does not materialize. Instead, they "double down" or re-double their efforts. In other words, once those who were earning $20,000 achieve their hoped-for $40,000 goal, they then raise the bar and believe that it will now take about $80,000 to be happy. We know students who have recalibrated their "happiness" number through four cycles of goal-setting. They have multiplied their original incomes by a factor of more than 100, and they are still fixated on a moving target.

LIVING IN THE PROSPERITY ZONE

How do you know you're living in the Prosperity Zone? Here are some good clues. There is alignment between how you are earning a living and your core. You have "stretch goals," but they are based on the confidence that comes from focusing on what you have instead of what you lack. You are making steady progress in growing your income so that you can fund your lifestyle and still have something left over to save, invest, or give away. You are happy because your happiness corresponds with your values, talents, and passions. You have systems in place to support you. You celebrate the victories, big and small, as you fix your sights on your Polaris Point.

We hope you have enjoyed this glimpse of what's possible. You can be a visitor or take up permanent residency, but we hope you unpack your bags and stay. You belong here.

Giving Back

One way you know you're truly in the Prosperity Zone is that it becomes not only possible but essential to give significant chunks of it away. Call it what you will: giving back, philanthropy, charitable giving, tithing, or establishing a foundation. By whatever name, it seems to be a common element among those whom we most celebrate for living in the Prosperity Zone. It is indeed a paradox that a core tenant of sustainable prosperity is to give much of it away.

Randy's Story *Money was pretty tight in the years before I was to go to college. My parents were both high school teachers and valued education highly, but they made it clear to me that if I wanted to go to college, I would have to find a way to pay for it myself. That proved very difficult, so for a couple of years right after high school, I did some volunteer work in the Philippines. It was an amazing experience, and I learned a lot about how some people get by with much less than I had growing up.*

When I got back to the United States and started to apply for colleges, I still didn't know how I would pay for it. I supposed I would apply for scholarships and, failing that, take out student loans and get a part time job. But then my grandmother, who had passed away about five years previously, made her presence felt. It turns out my grandmother had saved $3,000 for each of her grandchildren to help them go to college. Unbeknownst to me, the money had just been sitting in an account waiting for the day I went to college. I can't even express how overwhelmed I was to learn what a difference my grandmother's quiet generosity made in my life. My mother told me what her mother said: "I don't need this money. I want to make sure I can bless the lives of my posterity and those who want to excel and do great things." I look at her example, and it inspires me to be generous. I can't repay my grandmother, but I can pay it forward to others. The best way for us to repay the past is to put the future in debt to ourselves.

LIVE IN YOUR PROSPERITY ZONE

Prosperity Steps

Your Prosperity Zone is the place where what you love to do more than anything in the whole world also makes you money. You are truly in the zone when what makes you money makes you and other people happy and when work doesn't seem like work at all. You occupy the Prosperity Zone when you are able to find balance between the happiness you want and the money you earn.

Complete this Prosperity Step online at www.prosperbook.com/PS2.

Are you currently living in the Prosperity Zone? Can you answer "yes" to the following questions?

1. Is there alignment between how you are earning a living and your core?
2. Are your "stretch goals" based on the confidence that comes from focusing on what you have instead of desperation over what you lack?
3. Are you making steady progress in growing your income so that you can fund your lifestyle and still have something left over to save? Invest? Give away?
4. Are you happy because your happiness corresponds with your values, talents, and passions?
5. Do you have systems or networks in place to support you?
6. Do you celebrate the victories, big and small, as you fix your sights on your Polaris Point?

7. Are you giving chunks of your prosperity away to create value and better the lives of others?

MONEY + HAPPINESS + SUSTAINABILITY = PROSPERITY

Prosperity can be a process, and some may find it difficult to recognize when they start to live in the Prosperity Zone. Sometimes our lives drift in and out of prosperity because of a lack of sustainability. Help yourself stay in the zone by knowing what it takes to truly be prosperous. How many of the following questions can you reply "yes" to?

Money

1. Is your financial outlook positive?
2. Do you have excess after all of your financial obligations are met?
3. Do you enjoy what you do for income?
4. Do you feel like your income is aligned with your passion?
5. Are you on track to make more money this year than last year?
6. Do you feel like you are thriving? (Or just surviving?)

Happiness

1. Are you generally happy with your current place in life and where you are heading?
2. Do you know where you are heading?
3. Do you feel like you are moving forward? (Or backward/stagnant?)
4. Are you happy about the different facets of your life? (Personal, Family, Career, Physical, and Financial?)
5. Do you have a positive personal image and live with your own "personal vibe"?

6. Are you able to be happy for others when they experience success?

Sustainability

1. Do you feel like you are growing personally, professionally, and financially?
2. Are you able to share and give away some of your prosperity?
3. Are you joyfully and deliberately celebrating life and all your victories?
4. Do you have a long-term plan to grow your current happiness and wealth?
5. Have you diversified your income sources?
6. Do you evaluate your Polaris Point often and make proper adjustments to your course?

CHAPTER 3

EARN FROM YOUR CORE

Where your talents and the needs of the world cross
lies your calling.

—Aristotle

Your core consists of three elements: your values, your sense of purpose, and your unique set of abilities, talents, and passions. The third prosperity practice aligns your earning opportunities with these elements of who you are and suggests ways you can extract sustainable value from your core.

Passion and profit actually mix. It is possible to get an income stream from what motivates you the most. The old saying is accurate: if you love what you do, you will never work another day in your life. The secret to prosperity is already within you. We believe you already have a unique set of talents and attributes that allows you to address in your own way the problems important to other people. That's your core. And here's the beautiful part. People whose problems you solve will be eager to pay you. That's what you earn. When you earn from your core, you are on the way to sustainable prosperity.

Your core is the sum of all those things that give life most meaning for you. Your core values are expressed everywhere. What's the first thing you think of when you wake up? What's the last thing you think about when you fall asleep? Frequently these are clues to what's most important. What are your hobbies and interests? Where in the world are you most energized? Most relaxed? In what areas do people look to you for advice and assistance?

The society we live in doesn't make it easy for us to recognize our core values or gifts. Introspection is often mistaken for self-absorption. It's easier to toss off "That's just the way I am" than to do the hard work of unpacking the particulars of what's hidden in the statement. Sometimes it's actually easier to recognize the core values in large groups of people than individuals. Think of nations. What's the core value of the United States? Maybe you said freedom or democracy. How about Switzerland? A lot of people say precision. Italy? Common responses are food or art. Now, what is the first thing people say about you?

What we coach our students to do is to be so aware and aligned with their core values that the people around them can instantly identify the values they stand for. The other word for this instant clarity about something is the *brand*.

STORIES FROM EARN FROM YOUR CORE

Earning from your core practice is unique to each individual because it always flows out of each individual's specific circumstances. To illustrate this point, we asked two individuals who came to Prosper for one-on-one education and coaching to describe their circumstances and the process that had led them to earn from their cores. The stories of these two students, told in their own voices, underscore the organizing power of the practice of earning from your core.

Dan Gazaway, "Pitching Academy" *I always wanted to be successful, perhaps as an entrepreneur, but I also knew in my heart that I wanted to enjoy the work, whatever I chose as my career. It took some time for me* to find the balance between work and happiness. Although I graduated from college with a teaching degree in health education, I knew right away that it wasn't the direction I wanted to go. My first job was selling weight equipment to school districts. I had about five sales jobs in eight years. I liked selling and was good at communicating with my customers. That gave me confidence that I could be a successful entrepreneur.

But what kind of business could I start? I was stuck until I met a fellow salesperson who had a successful side business. I peppered him with questions. He finally looked at me and asked me a simple question: "Dan, what are you really good at?"

I answered without hesitation. "The only thing I'm really good at is baseball."

He smiled and said, "Well, that's great. Where did you go to get your training and knowledge about baseball?"

I told him that when I was younger I had attended a number of pitching seminars and clinics that brought in Major League pitchers such as Nolan Ryan and Randy Johnson to share their skills and insights. He encouraged me to consider a business based on my passion for pitching. Later, I recognized that this was the "Earn from Your Core" prosperity practice. Based on that exchange, I started the process that led to my opening my own pitching academy.

The answer had always been staring me in the face. It took somebody to just tell me to trust myself and give it a shot. Isn't that how every successful business starts?

As soon as I got home from that sales trip, I picked up three baseballs and went down to the local ball field. I noticed a dad playing catch with his son. I started a conversation, and we talked for a few minutes before I said, "Hey, I'm a pitching instructor. This is what I do. Do you mind if I spend a few minutes here with your son, helping him out?" They were both excited about it, and I worked with the son on his throw. Within ten minutes, the boy was throwing with more accuracy and velocity, and he *and his dad were really excited about it. It just felt so good to do what I loved and help someone else.*

I didn't expect to earn anything that day, but before they went home the dad pressed $50 into my hand. It was the easiest and most joyful $50 I have ever made. It didn't feel like work at all, because it wasn't work. My business just blossomed from there, and soon I was giving pitching lessons every day. After much success in giving individual pitching lessons, I wanted to scale up the business to generate passive income using the Internet. The result was an online portal that aggregates a number of books, training videos, and educational materials about pitchers and pitching.

Now I get daily consistent income that doesn't depend on me giving individual lessons. It's a good feeling to wake up each morning and check my e-mail to see that I've already had some earnings for the day.

My Polaris Point? It goes something like this: My passion is baseball. I can look at a pitcher, and after watching one or two pitches I can tell right away what they need to work on. People are going to see that passion, and they are going to be drawn to it. My goal is to combine my baseball passion with my talents for communicating, coaching, and helping others. I will be doing a disservice if I don't use those passions and talents like I'm supposed to.

Jennifer, "Fit Mamas"

Jennifer came to us a few years ago. She had worked in the business world and then as a trainer/instructor at a fitness club, but when she started her family, her priorities changed. She was eager to make a financial contribution but wanted total control over her hours. She concluded that meant a Web-based business she could do from home at times of her choosing. She came to us for coaching because, while she had a general idea of her economic goals, Jennifer felt she needed help in deciding what her strengths were, what specific business to pursue, and how to acquire the skills to succeed. In other words, she needed to determine her core and how to earn from it.

The first few coaching sessions focused on assisting Jennifer to identify which of her passions she most wanted to pursue. Under the direction of Andrew, Jennifer's coach, she talked about what really got her excited about life. Her core readily emerged: Jennifer was passionate about physical fitness, writing, and parenting. With Andrew's coaching, Jennifer soon formulated a plan. She would create and sell a series of fitness videos targeted to new mothers to help them get back into shape after giving birth.

The next challenge was to determine a viable business model that would allow her to earn money by transforming these passions into a business.

Jennifer's Story *I am the owner of a business called "Fit Mamas." My whole goal is to become a fitness guru in women's fitness, pregnancy, and new moms. My main product is a stroller workout in which I teach moms how to get back their bodies by combining drills while they are out walking with the baby in the stroller.*

I'm now working my dream. Shortly after producing my DVD, I began doing monthly fitness segments on the local news. I secured sponsorship from an upscale fitness clothing line. Then I landed a segment on a Home Shopping Network TV show. I believe that the universe is really supporting my passion for helping women. I'm amazed that people want to help me, too. All these creative, amazing people are coming together to help me make my business a success. Now I feel that I can reach my ultimate dream, which is to help women all over the world reach their optimum potential in body, mind, and spirit.

YOUR PERSONAL VIBE

Some people call it branding. We say it's crafting your personal vibe: the thing that sets you apart and makes you unique. Formulating your personal vibe is critical because it serves as the basis for everything that connects people to you rationally, emotionally, and commercially. An effective personal vibe, one that is aligned with and reflects your core values, rests on three foundations: authenticity, consistency, and clarity.

Most of our students understand the vital importance of differentiating themselves, but the single biggest mistake they make is to grasp for whatever seems to them the most popular or expedient. So they jump on the brand du jour that received the most tweets on Twitter that month. Or they try on identities that well-meaning people around them suggest they should try. But unless their personal vibe is from the core—if they fail to invest time in aligning the identity they present to the world—their efforts will backfire. Remember, the key to prosperity is to be compensated based on your core.

The good news is you have the power to craft your personal vibe into exactly what you want it to be. It's not even that difficult. All it requires is that you make your intentions clear, act consistently in the service of your core talents, and speak up. When you do that, we guarantee people will notice, they will tell others, and your personal vibe will thrive precisely because you do.

SEEK OUT PROBLEMS

The best way to start a profitable business or move up in a company is to find a problem and create a solution for it. A solution is reframing a perceived challenge into a strength. In the workplace, such reframing is powerful because everyone is usually focused only on the problem. But if you focus on the solution and implement it, you are suddenly seen as a hero. The trick is to identify a set of solutions that you can address from your core. Here are some tactics to help you do that.

Find and Align

Identify those businesses or service providers that are being paid to do what you are naturally good at. Find people, occupations, associations, and groups who are involved in doing what your core tells you to do. Join, volunteer, or partner with those groups. If you do so, you enthusiasm will be noticed, and your reputation will begin.

When he came to us for coaching, Joe had a background in real estate and construction. He was especially passionate about the decorative possibilities of concrete. With the help of his coach, he quickly zeroed in on how to earn from his core: Joe established a business to design, fabricate, and sell decorative concrete products to homeowners, small to midsized commercial contractors, and property managers. He further distinguished his business by specializing in projects that were typically too small for commercial contractors to undertake. His expertise identified a slice of the business that he could serve without as much competition. We were delighted when Joe told us that within six months of launching the business he was making $20,000 per month.

Here's an example of someone learning to earn from their core in their current organization, an employee in our own organization. Early on in our business, we were expanding at a rate that was frankly out of control. We certainly didn't have the organizational infrastructure to keep up with the demands of the growing business. Our core was helping people, not administration, so this development was probably not a surprise to anyone. But then we received help from a most unexpected corner of our company. One of our newly hired customer service representatives, 23-year-old Jade Koyle, had been a home-schooled farm boy who up to then had distinguished himself mostly by his uncanny way with farm machinery. As it turned out, he had an amazing knack for making complicated problems seem simple as well.

Jade saw how we were struggling, and he came to us with a few suggestions. At first, we were skeptical and resisted, but Jade's clarity and ownership of the problem earned our trust. He then implemented the solution he'd proposed, and it worked! He developed one of the most advanced technology platforms a business could hope for, and Jade became one of our most trusted and strategic partners. Today, he is our chief marketing officer, with line responsibility over millions of dollars of assets.

Shine the Stone

It's great when you know what your core is. Your core is like a stone—it will serve you well, but only if you polish it and let everyone else see it shine. Your goal is to polish this stone: to learn skills, to enhance your abilities, and, through practice, to develop your innate potential to unprecedented levels of achievement. In other words, you need to become an expert in whatever it is you have chosen to do. Here's where the 10,000-hour rule comes in. Made popular in Malcolm Gladwell's 2008 book *Outliers*, the 10,000-hour rule was derived from a study by Anders Ericsson, a psychologist who researched the success of violinists at the Berlin Academy of Music. In his study, he found that in every case the violinists that performed the best spent more time practicing. Gladwell further describes how the magic number of 10,000 hours was the average number of hours the violinists, as well as athletes, composers, writers, artists, even criminals, spent to achieve their success. Here are two steps to start benefitting from the 10,000-hour rule.

Do the Math. Ten thousand hours is about three hours a day over ten years. Yes, ten years may seem like a long time, but that is why the first step is so important. Spending this kind of time on your passion will not feel like work, nor will it feel like ten years. One of our coaching students was skeptical. He was in late middle age, recently laid off from a job, and looking to start a new business. "Ten years is too long," he complained. "If I invest that much effort into building that expertise, I'll be 65 years old." Our response was direct: "And how old will you be if you don't invest the effort?" He did the work, developed a world-class capability in his business, and prospered.

First Be the Best. Television executive Grant Tinker was asked how he planned to make NBC number one. His response: "First we will be the best, and then we will be the first." And that's what happened. In the years he was president, Tinker's focus on quality programming led to audience growth and profits.

Ask for Some of the Value You Create

Once you know what people are being paid to do, learn from them, apprentice with them, allow them to coach you, learn the key skills to monetize the ability, and then ask for your share. Understand how to create the value and build a business around it, and capture some of that value. Many people we work with are already creating value doing what they love, but they do not ask for compensation. You will be surprised how much people are willing to pay you.

Earning from your core is intrinsically satisfying. It can take many forms. For some people, it's about putting happiness first by being able to earn a living by doing what they love, whether that's music, creating a Web site, or white-water rafting. For others, it's about balancing work with family commitments. But for most people, earning from your core is about making sufficient money. So that begs an important question: how do you measure what's sufficient?

WHAT'S YOUR YARDSTICK?

Earning from your core requires you to choose a yardstick so you know you're on the right track. What yardstick will you use to measure your prosperity? Making money is certainly one measure. Having influence or prestige is another. But there are other yardsticks available. Harvard Business School Professor Clayton Christensen recently recalibrated the measure that he now applies to his own life and sense of prosperity.

After being diagnosed with cancer and faced with the possibility that his life would end sooner than he'd planned, Christensen said, "I have a pretty clear idea of how my ideas have generated enormous revenue for companies that have used my research; I know I've had a substantial impact. But as I've confronted this disease, it's been interesting to see how unimportant that impact is to me now. I've concluded that the metric by which God will assess my life isn't dollars but the individual people whose lives I've touched."

We hope you will be spared such a health crisis, but we believe that we all benefit from taking a good hard look at the yardsticks we use. It may be that, in the end, many of us will come to question some of the yardsticks we use and we will worry less, for example, about the level of individual prominence we have achieved. We have noticed that humility is a characteristic common to the people who have achieved the highest levels of sustainable prosperity. Humility is not thinking less of yourself; it's thinking of yourself less often. Think about the yardstick by which your life will be judged, and make a resolution to live every day so that in the end your life will be judged a success.

EARN FROM YOUR CORE

Prosperity Steps

Your core aligns your earning opportunities with the elements of who you are and suggests ways you can extract sustainable value from your core. Passion and profit actually mix. It is possible to get an income stream from what motivates you the most.

Complete this Prosperity Step online at www.prosperbook.com/PS3.

Take a few minutes to write out the answers to these questions:

1. What is your definition of your core, in thirty words or less?
2. Name five enterprises/businesses aligned with your passion and core. What are their business models? Which ones offer the most value or reward?
3. How can you be the best at doing this? What will make you different, better, and special? What will be your personal vibe?
4. How will you be compensated? What is your yardstick to measure success?

CHAPTER 4

START WITH WHAT YOU ALREADY HAVE

The best things in Life are yours if you can appreciate yourself.

—Dale Carnegie

Li'l Abner was a very popular comic strip in the 1950s. A scene in the movie based on the comic strip illustrates why we think Starting with What You Already Have should be the very first prosperity principle. Li'l Abner is lazily fishing with a group of friends when someone asks him, "Say, Abner, if you could be anyone else in the whole world, who'd you druther be?"

ABNER: Me.

FRIEND: Jus' you?

ABNER: Jus' me.

FRIEND: What's so special 'bout being you?

ABNER: Ain't nuthin' special about it, it's just so handy, that's all.

In other words, you may as well be yourself because everyone else is already taken.

Li'l Abner didn't have much to his name, and we would have understood if he had named a movie star or famous athlete. But he instinctively appreciated the first practice of prosperity.

THE POWER OF FOCUSING ON WHAT
YOU ALREADY HAVE

An amazing thing happens in the confidence, creativity, and outlook when people realize they do not need to wait for outside circumstances to change before they can succeed. Understanding that what you bring to the market, your company, and in general the world is only something you can bring. Your unique prosperity fingerprint can solve problems and create value in a way that only you can. Start with that, build on it, and you will be shocked at the power you can already wield.

As screenwriters go, Sandy was successful. He had sold a number of scripts. An independent movie he had written some years earlier was doing modestly well at the box office. But when he came to us, Sandy was in despair. For over a year, he had been trying to write something but nothing came. "I'm empty," he told us. "I don't have anything to work with." It seemed to us a classic case of writer's block. He agreed to try some coaching to find his way through this period of frustration, whatever it was.

For their first session, the coach asked Sandy to close his eyes and focus on the things he had that he was grateful for. Then nothing. The silence was deafening. In general, coaches try not to prompt students, but Sandy was so lost he needed a hand. The coach kept it light.

Coach *How about the beach?*

Sandy *The beach? Yeah, I like walking on the beach.*

Coach *You have a nice computer.*

Sandy *That's true. I got a good deal on it.*

Coach *What about your cat?*

Sandy *OK, I'm grateful for my cat.*

Coach *And the moon?*

Sandy *I love when the moon is full.*

And so the logjam was broken. Over the next few sessions, Sandy made a list of all the things he had going for him: his family, friends, professional achievements, and respect from his peers. A few days after that, the writer woke up from a deep sleep with an idea for a scene.

Sometimes when we shift our emphasis from what we are lacking (ideas, employment, relationships, etc.) to what we have (nature's abundance, loyal pets, full moons, etc.), something within us shifts. When we least expect it, when we are most quiet, our creative unconscious can be heard. Have you ever noticed that great solutions to problems you've been struggling with tend to arrive while you are taking a shower or biking or when you're otherwise relaxed? No one, not even Sandy, can know for a certainty how these things happen. But Sandy told us he got out of bed, fired up his notebook computer, and before the sun had slipped over the horizon, he had half a screenplay framed out. Six weeks later, the script was finished. Within the month, four film studios were bidding to buy it.

BEST OUTCOMES

We have seen thousands of students go through our program on the path to prosperity. We've noticed that the students with the best outcomes all had one thing in common: they started by focusing on the assets they already enjoyed rather than on what they lacked. It is not the case that the most successful students started with the most. As we stated in the introduction, the fullness of their plates when they started mattered less than the fact that, however little their plates contained, they noticed that their plates weren't empty. Whether they started with a lot or a little, those who emphasized what they had at the start tended to end up with the most.

This result was very curious to us, so we took a closer look.

There are two kinds of people in the world. There are those who spend all their time thinking about their limitations and deficits, and those who may be painfully aware of their weaknesses but choose instead to focus on what they do have. The second group of people have a smoother ride on the road to prosperity.

It's not hard to see why. The first group spends much of their energy thinking about how to overcome their weaknesses. The second group invests their energy in enhancing their existing gifts and assets, humble as they may be. Which group of people would you rather work with, mentor, or rely on?

The problem is that focusing on negative thoughts actually re-wires our minds in a way that sabotages our sincere efforts. It's not too surprising that many of us have the problem of fixating on what we don't have. We live in a consumer culture that bombards us with thousands of commercial messages designed to persuade us that we are not attractive enough, smart enough, or successful enough. It's no wonder that we unconsciously focus more on what we lack, what we fear, or what we're trying to avoid than on what we have.

We see this attitude in our coaching every day. Starting a coaching engagement is pretty straightforward. Our coaches always ask students a variation of the question: What do you want? In the beginning, many of our students have a hard time telling us what they *want*. For example, we hear many goals such as these:

I don't want to worry about mortgage payments anymore.

I've been trying my whole life to be an accountant like my dad, and now I just want to be me, and I need help.

I don't want to wake up with a bad feeling in the pit in my stomach thinking about working with my boss.

I need someone to help me stop spinning my wheels so I can get rich.

It would be great if my managers had respect for me so I could get a decent promotion.

You see where we're going with this? It's much easier for many students to tell us what they don't want.

As we followed their progress, we saw that a majority of these students either failed to complete the program or had lackluster results. We believe a big part of the problem is that these students placed their focus on what they didn't want. And since we get more of what we focus on, what do you think tends to happen?

- They don't want mortgage payments, but mortgage payments seem to persist.
- They don't want to feel like a loser, but they tend to keep on losing.
- They want to stop spinning their wheels, but the wheels tend to spin.
- They don't want their boss to disrespect them, yet they don't respect themselves.

WHERE DO I START?

The goal is to make money from your core strengths and abilities. That's the key goal. So when a Prosper student asks, "Where do I start?" this is what we say.

First, look around and see how other people or businesses are generating income from a core that's identical (or similar) to your own. For example, if your core is a passion and aptitude for mathematics, list ten ways you see others making money from these skills. There are lots of ways to do that. Start with Google and search for "careers in mathematics." Or go to the Web site of the American Mathematics Society and check out the job listings. Some of the insights will be obvious: math teacher, physicist, or accountant. But you may be surprised at the unexpected jobs or opportunities that require proficiency in math, such as currency trading. Based on the ideas you generate, the next step is to use a model that is obviously working for someone else. If it works for them, it will probably work for you. Of course, you must then customize the model to fit your unique circumstances or create a variation to the proven model to differentiate yourself in the market. You can then start to create some real income from your core.

We Get More of What We Focus On

What happens when you buy your dream car—let's say it happens to be deep red—and you start to drive it around? If you guessed that you would suddenly see red cars everywhere you drive, you'd probably be right. What's going on here? Are there suddenly more red cars on the highway just because you purchased one?

Of course not. You're simply focusing more on red cars. As Laura Goodrich points out in *Seeing Red Cars: Driving Yourself, Your Team, and Your Organization to a Positive Future,* you get more of whatever you focus on. Drawing on the latest scientific research, Goodrich has shown that by concentrating on the "I wants" that best fit your passions and interests, both personal and professional, and then by finding support, managing weaknesses, setting priorities, and developing action plans to achieve them, you have the best shot at transforming those wants into reality. This is true whether what you want is better health, a more fulfilling job, or a business that you have created.

If you're focused on red cars, you will notice more red cars. If you're focused on becoming a person who has prosperity, you will notice more opportunities to act on that desire. You will be attentive to conversations at parties. You will be more inclined to ask a question or introduce yourself. You will be more attentive to stories about prosperity on television or articles about prosperity while you are waiting at the dentist's office. Will paying attention to prosperity create the prosperity you seek? Not by itself. To gain anything from that kind of focus requires you to recognize an opportunity, make a decision, and take decisive action.

Here's another example. When you are focused on becoming a healthy and energetic person instead of focusing on avoiding becoming an overweight person, you'll start to notice different things. Your attention will be pulled to notice posters about fitness centers or hiking activities or healthy eating classes. You will find inner resources and ideas that didn't arise—or you didn't notice—when you focused on your extra weight.

At the very start of this book, we invited you to take the free Prosperity Assessment at www.prosperbook.com/profile. Now that you are more than halfway through the Prosperity Practices, it might be a good time to take it again. Compare the two results to determine how your profile has shifted. It will give you important clues going forward and allow you to make even better use of the lessons we describe. If you skipped taking the Assessment, we encourage you to take it now.

Take time to know who you are. What's negotiable and what's not? These reveal your values. A big part of this commitment is to stop trying to be somebody else.

Ethan's Story *When I did my volunteer work in Brazil, I looked up the leader who supervised all the volunteer teams in Brazil. His leadership style was authoritarian. "Do this," he would say, "and then do the other thing." I felt he had the answers for everything. At one point during my mission, I was put in charge of a team, and I tried to lead by his example. Bad idea. It quickly became obvious that I had to find another way to lead. For one thing, I didn't have all the answers, and it was no use pretending that I did. What I found out about myself was that instead of being the guy with the answers, my real strength was building teams around me who did know the answers and then supporting them so they would have the most opportunities to create influence and collaborations. That's when I felt I was able to drive things forward, and this allowed me to build larger teams based on collaboration.*

You need to be you. Unless you take this step, income may come and go, but financial security will stay elusive. Prosperity is simply not sustainable unless the business or career you build has a foundation solidified by your unique strengths, interests, and values, all guided by your Polaris Point.

START WITH WHAT YOU ALREADY HAVE

Prosperity Steps

Every company maintains an inventory of its assets. We suggest you do the same, because taking stock of your personal assets is the first step on the path to prosperity. Inventory the assets you already have. Start with your unique strengths and competencies. What are some of your natural talents? What comes so easily you often don't even notice it? Sometimes we have talents we don't appreciate as talents that we worked for. How about the acquired skills you have used successfully? Your work experiences? Don't forget your life experiences. Much of your hard-won perspective comes as a result of the challenges you have overcome. Then list your talents, passions, and deeply held values. These are assets, too.

Complete this Prosperity Step online at www.prosperbook.com/PS4.

Inventing Your Assets

We've noticed that the students with the best outcomes all had one thing in common: they started by focusing on the assets they already enjoyed rather than on what they lacked. It is not the case that the most successful students started with the most. So in this exercise, please start making a list of the things (big and small) that you are most grateful for.

Next, create an inventory of your assets. Take a piece of paper, and create three columns with the following column titles:

Unique Life Experiences and Expertise	Unique Abilities, Talents, and Passions	Personal Contacts, Networks, and Business Connections

In each column, write down as many assets as you can think of. Take your time. This exercise requires some thinking. If you have trouble coming up with attributes, try shifting your point of view: imagine that your best friend (or favorite supervisor) is making the list on your behalf. What attributes would he or she list? For the third column, some people find it helpful to consult their Rolodex or address book. When you are done, study the assets in your inventory. They are probably more abundant than you thought.

CHAPTER 5

COMMIT TO YOUR PROSPERITY PATH

*Unless commitment is made, there are only promises
and hopes; but no plans.*

—*Peter Drucker*

So far, we have covered the following Prosperity Practices: Locate Your Polaris Point, Live in Your Prosperity Zone, Earn from Your Core, and Start with What You Already Have. We now want to help you pull it all together in a practice we call "Commit to Your Prosperity Path."

Experience has shown us that you cannot make a meaningful commitment to your Prosperity Path unless you understand this new direction in your mind and heart. If you put in the work up front in accurately defining your plan, then you can commit with confidence, knowing that prosperity will be the successful outcome.

Let us tell you a story about how we learned an important lesson about committing to a plan.

When our company had reached about 10,000 coaching students, we decided to invest in a sophisticated customer management (CRM) system. It wasn't cheap, but we wanted the best. We sat wide-eyed as the software demonstrator walked through all the wonderful bells and whistles this CRM system would give us. We were excited by the thought of all the ways we were going to be able to better serve our students by delivering even more personalized learning.

The software demonstrator could tell we had stars in our eyes. At this point, he stopped the presentation and asked us a question: "What do you think is the most important element to the success of this new CRM system?" In our excitement, we rattled off all the cool things we supposed the system would allow our company to do. Student progress reporting. Better understanding of the student experience. Real-time tracking.

But what the CRM software representative said next caught us by surprise, framed our expectations of the software in a new way, and probably saved everyone a lot of frustration. "Yes, those are great outputs of the software," he told us. "But they are not the most important elements to the success. The most important element for success is the accuracy of the information you enter into the system. The output you get from the software is only as good as the input."

Lesson learned.

We want to make sure that you can use these Six Prosperity Practices to create the outputs that will make a positive change in your life. To do that, we need to emphasize the importance of working with the proper inputs. To illustrate, first consider the Prosperity Blueprint of one of our students. Then we are going to invite you to create your own. You will be then better able to find the inputs that will guarantee optimum outputs in your path to prosperity.

PROSPERITY BLUEPRINT OF BRAD SIMMONS

Brad Simmons, one of our students, had a passion for being of assistance to disabled pets and their owners. When he came to us for help in making his dreams real, we asked him to create a Prosperity Plan based on our Six Prosperity Practices. He has allowed us to share his blueprint in our book.

Practice 1. My Polaris Point. *At the end of this process, I want to be a person who has invested time in what really matters. I want my wife Susan and daughter Missy to feel that they always come first. I want to earn money as a result of helping pet owners and animals enjoy a more satisfied life. In particular, I want to make a positive difference to the environment and animals, especially disabled animals. I want to help handicapped animals in particular to be better off because I was on the earth.*

Practice 2. My Prosperity Zone. *Money is not the major driver for me. I want to live my Polaris Point and make enough from this venture to pay at least what I am making as a bike manufacturer. I also want to employ my daughter Missy so we can work together and she can save for college. I will remember why I am doing this and keep my earnings in line with my Polaris Point. If I make more than that, I will stash it away for Susan and me to create memories together as we travel.*

Practice 3. Earn from My Core. *I have a unique ability to care for animals and understand the pain owners feel when their pets are disabled. My dog Sally was hit by a car and was disabled and died shortly after. As a bike manufacturer, I have skills to create a unique wheelchair for dogs. This invention will allow injured or disabled dogs to go on walks and enjoy a better life. Because of my unique design and its weight, it will be the ideal wheelchair for dogs. I will call my business "Hi-Tail It."*

Practice 4. Start with What I Already Have. *Through my many years of volunteer service, I have solid contacts with the many veterinarian hospitals in the area. I also know Adriana Silvia, who works at* Love Your Dog *magazine. She says she can get the magazine to run a story about my product and promote my company. I can also get the alloy metal and wheel supplies from my manufacturing vendors. I only have about ten hours a week, but I will start there. As sales grow, I will eventually transition to a full-time focus. Now that I know what I need to do to succeed, I will make an agreement with myself and keep to it.*

NOW IT'S YOUR TURN

It may appear that it was easy for Brad Simmons to generate those statements that make up his Prosperity Blueprint. That impression would be a mistake, and Brad would assure you that wasn't the case. The statements you see here came to him only after completing the exercises that we describe in this book. He first had to locate his Polaris Point, determine his Prosperity Zone, and plot his financial needs in terms of expenses and income. And after he completed the exercises, he took time to contemplate what it all meant. Then he worked hard to put everything in a tight narrative form that avoided extra words. Only based on doing the work was Brad able to move forward with confidence.

One of the precepts of the Prosperity Zone is that there are no shortcuts, no get-rich-quick schemes to prosperity. By the same token, there are no shortcuts to committing to your Prosperity Path.

Write Me Down, Make Me Real

A few of our students resist this practice, but most get that writing down their goals is a powerful expression of their commitment to actually achieve them. They understand that writing down their goals serves several useful outcomes. They accept that writing down their plan allows them to:

- Visualize their objective.
- Be specific about the target.
- Keep their goals visible as a continual reminder of their objectives.
- Focus on the milestones.
- Celebrate their progress when they review the plans.

Students ask us for suggestions on how to start this process and make it more powerful. Here's what we tell them.

Write It Out by Hand. We are firm believers in actually writing down all plans by hand because doing so seems to make the planning more concrete, infusing the plans with a kinesthetic physicality. Writing down the goals encourages a sense of accountability, as there is something very permanent about documenting one's intentions. Of course, some students prefer to create their plans digitally—whatever works. For us, we still believe there's something very intimate and empowering about committing one's goals to paper by hand.

Narrate It. We also suggest that students write down their goals in narrative form, not just as a list of bullet points or a spreadsheet. It's not enough to write, "I want to accomplish X." That's good as an intention, but it's not a plan. Everyone wants to accomplish one goal or another; everyone might want to eat healthier and exercise more. But merely writing down the intention, no matter how heartfelt, does nothing to empower you to actually accomplish it. The trick is to write down your goal as part of an empowering and very personal document that can be used to hold you accountable. In this way, the plan becomes a part of a coordinated strategy to transform that intention into actual results.

Memorize It. Commit as much of your plan to memory as you can. At the very least, come up with a thirty-word elevator speech version of your plan and memorize that. It's enormously empowering to be able to recite your plan every day. Memorization is a guardrail against the frustration that pursuing every worthwhile goal sometimes entails. When the going gets tough, the tough recite their plan, remind themselves of the goal, and re-decide to make it a priority.

Keep It Visible. Write the elevator speech or summary of your plan on an index card or sticky note, and put it on your bathroom mirror. Let it be the first thing you read every morning and the last thing you read every night.

Set Boundaries. The deals we've done are important, but the deals that are most important to us are those we haven't done. At times, saying no can be more productive then saying yes. You need to set boundaries in your life, because if you don't, other people will. Boundaries are imaginary lines that keep the actions of yourself and others from hurting, distracting, or imposing on you against your will. Boundaries are limits you set in advance on how you will act and how others are permitted to behave around you.

Honor Agreements. Agreements are the bread and butter of prosperity. Agreements are basically an exchange of promises with the intention of achieving an outcome desired by all parties. Clear agreements express a shared vision and how to get there.

YOU MUST BE PRESENT TO WIN

"Eighty percent of success is showing up," says Woody Allen. But what does it mean to show up, and how do our agreements help us show up for prosperity?

On the most literal level, "showing up" means making the effort to participate in some activity. Showing up means taking the meeting, attending the conference, accepting the invitation to be mentored, going to the networking event, or meeting a colleague for a drink. It means extending ourselves to do what we know to be in our interests, even if we feel tired or grumpy at a particular moment.

All this engagement with the physical world is essential. But by "showing up" we have something a little different in mind.

We're talking about being present from a place of authenticity. Showing up for prosperity goes well beyond the physical definition of showing up. It means answering the question, Who are you when you show up? In other words, who are you showing up as? Think about your core values, passions, talents, and abilities. What attracts people to you? What does your personal presence convey? Are you serious or playful? High energy? Curious? Cooperative? Aggressive? And how does that presence align with your vision of prosperity? Showing up as your authentic self, with the energy and passion you bring to your work, goes deeper than "walking the talk." It gives you the edge that allows you to stand out in a crowd.

Showing up is also about stretching yourself into situations that may be outside your comfort zone.

One of our coaching graduates recently started a business to train and provide personal trainers to fitness centers. Within a few months of opening his doors, he was approached by one of the largest chains of fitness centers to recruit, train, and manage hundreds of trainers in the western United States. The student confided to us that he didn't "feel quite ready" to take on such a complicated contract, but he was going to take his best shot anyway. He was willing to show up for the challenge and confront whatever fear he had. Maybe he'll get the project, or maybe he won't. Showing up means acknowledging that we might never feel quite ready for anything, but that we will nevertheless go for the big project, the big clients, the big deal.

When we show up big, big things tend to happen. The universe is not served by you showing up small.

KEEP YOUR WORD TO YOURSELF

It's one thing to keep your word. It's another to take an active role in what that word is.

Melissa was always rock solid at keeping her agreements. What-ever she was asked to do, she did with skill and attention to every detail. Her coworkers knew that if Melissa agreed to do something, they could consider it done. She worked for NASA, a large govern-ment agency, and spent her days completing with great profession-alism all the tasks she was assigned. But she was frustrated with a career that seemed limited and unsatisfying. She came to us for coaching.

After a few sessions, she got an important insight. Her ability to keep agreements was, indeed, a strength. But she learned that, so long as other people set the agenda, she would be frustrated. Only when it was Melissa deciding what needed to be done—when it was a matter of her own agreements that she was keeping—would she be fulfilled. Satisfaction for Melissa would come when the agreements she took on were in the service of her passion and need for independence. After going through our process, she zeroed in on her true core: dancing. Melissa loved ballet, modern dance, folk dance, and especially ballroom dance.

With a little coaching, Melissa launched a ballroom dancing Web site. Within eighteen months, she was earning enough to be able to quit her job and devote herself full time to her own business. She feels prosperous every time she celebrates that she was able to free herself from keeping the agreements she made to others in favor of agreements she made to herself.

COMMIT TO YOUR PROSPERITY PATH

Prosperity Steps

Experience has shown us that you cannot make a meaningful commitment to your Prosperity Path unless you understand this new direction in your mind and heart. If you put in the work up front in accurately defining your plan, then you can commit with confidence, knowing that prosperity will be the successful outcome.

Complete your Prosperity Path by responding to these statements online at www.prosperbook.com/PS5.

Memorize the responses if you can.

My Polaris Point Is:

I Intend to Earn from My Core by:

I Will Start with What I Have by:

Additional Prosperity Questions:

1. What problem am I trying to solve?
2. What is it that I am selling or offering?
3. What is my distribution channel?
4. How am I going to let people know what I am offering?
5. Who is my target customer?
6. How much are people willing to pay for a solution to this problem?

7. What offers similar to mine are already available?
8. What makes my offer better, unique, special?
9. How will I articulate my solution to the customers?

Here Are the Reasons *Why* I Want Prosperity:

Prosperity Visualization

Imagine that you have come across an old friend you haven't seen in five years. Your friend is delighted to see you and wants to catch up. He has a number of questions. Please answer your friend's questions as you imagine you will answer them in five years.

1. Where do you now live?
2. What kind of car do you drive?
3. How are you supporting yourself?
4. How much are you earning?
5. What are the hobbies you actively pursue?
6. Where was the last place you took a two-week vacation?

Prosperity Goals

Everyone needs goals. Your goals are what you want to achieve, reach, get to, or accomplish. Without goals, it is difficult to have a sense of direction and achievement. Let's see what your goals are.

My goals for . . .

Today:

Tomorrow:

Next week:

Next month:

Next year:

The year after:

Three years from now:

Five years from now:

Ten years from now:

Prosperity Path Agreement

I, _____, hereby commit to the achievement of my Prosperity Path. I agree to set strong boundaries, to "show up" and "be present." I understand that I need to hold myself accountable for my actions because "if it's to be, it's up to me." I agree to commit at least 5 to 10 hours per week to developing my future prosperity. I will pledge to take action in creating the life I truly want and to uphold the values I stand for. I promise to recognize the abundance I already have while achieving my goals along my Prosperity Path. I understand that with the expectation of new results in my life comes an expectation of new actions. I commit fully to these required actions in the fulfillment of my goals.

_____   _____

Full Name (Signature)   Date

CHAPTER 6

TAKE PROFOUND ACTION

The vision must be followed by the venture.
It is not enough to stare up the steps—we must
step up the stairs.

—*Vance Havner*

Here's a riddle. There are five frogs sitting on a log. Four decide to jump off. How many frogs remain on the log?

Answer: All five. Four frogs may have decided to jump, but until they actually took action and jumped, the frogs stayed put.

The sixth Prosperity Practice recognizes that even world-class planning is irrelevant unless it is transformed into action. Decision is critical. Nothing happens without a decision. But guess what? Nothing happens with a decision unless it is followed by what we call Profound Action.

Profound Action is not just any action. By Profound Action, we mean action that has three elements. First, it is supportive of the decision. Second, it is aligned with your core values and passions. And third, it is consistent with your Polaris Point.

Even the Finest Decision Is Ineffective If It's Left to Collect Dust. Once you've made a decision, don't set it aside. Doing so will only work against the power of that decision. Instead, put the decision to work. Begin *without delay* to implement your decision. You have the knowledge, skills, and imagination to reach your goals. By this time, you've done the introspection and have gathered specialized knowledge. You have your network in place. You know you have the desire to make it happen. You have all the tools you need to take effective prosperous action.

HOW TO TAKE PROFOUND ACTION

A man approached the fabulously wealthy financier J. P. Morgan, and said, "Mr. Morgan, in this envelope I hold the guaranteed formula for success which I will gladly sell you for 25,000 dollars." "Sir," J. P. Morgan replied, "I do not know what it is in the envelope, but if you show it to me and I like it, I give you my word as a gentleman that I will pay you what you ask."

The man agreed to J. P. Morgan's terms, and handed over the envelope. J. P. Morgan opened it, and extracted a single sheet of paper. He gave it a quick look, put it back in the envelope, and paid the agreed-upon $25,000. The contents of the note:

1. Every morning, write down a list of the things that need to be done that day.
2. Do them.

Why did J. P. Morgan agree to pay $25,000 for advice that is so obvious? Because he understood that old habits die hard and that making a commitment to a new path requires discipline and even sacrifice. Nothing sharpens our discipline as much as paying for it. What is it about human nature that makes us value more what we pay for most dearly? The following story illustrates what we mean.

There was once a wise man walking down an ancient road when he was confronted by a samurai warrior. Drawing his sword, the samurai said, "Who are you? Where are you going? Why are you going there?" Unfazed, the wise man simply asked, "How much does your master pay you?" The samurai was taken aback by the lack of fear in the wise man's voice. "Two gold coins a month," he responded. The wise man reflected for a moment and then said, "I have a proposal for you. I'll pay you three gold coins per month if you stop me at this spot on the ancient road each month and challenge me to respond to those same three questions."

This is a story of revealing the authentic you, the first of the Six Prosperity Practices that we believe are key to a life of sustainable prosperity. How much more assured would our path to prosperity be if each of us had someone we could depend on to confront us with life's tough questions and not be satisfied with easy answers?

How much are you prepared to pay for lessons that will allow you to take the Profound Action that will turn your life in the right direction?

We get a lot of questions from people who don't like the way their lives are going. They tell us they could be more successful if only the economy were better, their boss weren't so mean, or their partners weren't so short-sighted. How often have you heard the phrase "You've got to play the hand that life dealt you"? We believe that the road to prosperity starts when you realize that you are the dealer. The best way to predict the future is to create it.

Our coaching starts with helping our students realize that while the problem may seem to be "out there," the real problem is actually much closer to home. The experience of our students is, to a great extent, completely scripted by the beliefs and thoughts that they repeat every day. The beliefs they have about careers, family, relationships, and especially money are the scripts that determine their lives. One of the first goals of coaching is to help students challenge the notion that these limitations are just the cards they've been dealt; they must accept, instead, that these beliefs are cards that they have systematically dealt to themselves. The second goal is to get students to say, "This is my creation, all of it. What I created, I have the power to change."

We don't pretend this is easy. There are reasons why our students came to accept such limitations. Dismantling these limiting beliefs requires replacing them with a set of more empowering beliefs. This step requires that students ask a very difficult question: "What must I believe about myself and the way I engage with this area of my life to make it the way I want?" If they want to change the outcome, they have to change the underlying beliefs that may be limiting them.

Commit to Continuous Action

Continuous action moves from your core and keeps you on your path. It ties all that you do together.

Say "Yes" to "No." Sometimes taking Profound Action means saying "no." Making a commitment to one course of action means saying "no" to others, some of which may at the time appear more attractive than the course you've chosen. But saying "yes" to everything effectively means saying "yes" to nothing. That's why it's so important for action to flow from your core values and passions. Aligning with your core serves to light the path you are on, making the footing more certain. The side roads will suddenly look less attractive. It's good to be flexible—we don't advocate blindly pursuing the path into a ditch just because your choice seemingly dictates it. We urge students to base their decisions on the evidence. But in the absence of evidence, keeping your eyes on the prize is the way to go.

Move Quickly. Hesitation is the enemy of Profound Action. We coach our students to move quickly and efficiently. The goal is to get into a flow that allows you to put your entire mental and physical self into the task. When this happens, discipline and clarity increase. You will enjoy the process, and the whole enterprise will feel less like work, more like passion. All this will happen when you move quickly and efficiently toward your goals.

Have Faith in Yourself. Faith is one of those words that mean so much to some people and so little to others. For us, faith is a huge part of our own prosperity. Many of our students also find that they can harness their faith to their goals. Like us, they acknowledge a connection to something larger than themselves. A few of our students have rolled their eyes at the supposed spiritual nature of the prosperity journey, but in our experience, most are simply not sure about the role that faith plays. They secretly worry that if they don't have enough faith—if they don't believe in the right things or fail to chant the magic words—they will not meet their goals and it will be their own fault for not believing enough.

We want to reassure readers that faith doesn't work like that. Faith in a higher power gives many people a significant boost, but faith by itself is no sure road to success. Rather, the faith we are talking about is the faith that proclaims that you already have everything you need to attain all that you desire. In other words, you are enough. If nothing else, can you have faith in that? From our perspective, as far as faith is concerned, here's the bottom line: your decisions and actions will be much more effective when they are based in faith in yourself than when they are based in doubt. Hope is as important as faith. We have hope that there is something better before we can or want to have faith in it.

Have the Courage to Stick to Your Decision. Whatever you decide, there will be other people who will challenge your decision. In fact, the more revolutionary and courageous your action, the more people will question your course. It may be tempting at the time to buy into that hesitation, so this is where courage and clarity come in. Courage is the willingness to go against the grain. Clarity is the ability to keep your eyes on your Polaris Point despite all the distractions.

Don't Turn Back. One of the elements of Profound Actions is that they are made in such a way that there's no going back. Action that is easily reversible is rarely the most effective.

PROSPERITY PARTNERS

While it's important to have the confidence to ignore outside influences, it's also useful to know when to ask for advice. No one can do it alone. One of the keys elements of starting with what you already have is to enlist the key people in your network who can inspire, guide, help, and mentor you. We call these people Prosperity Partners. Napoleon Hill calls them mastermind groups. By whatever name and however you organize them, these are the people who get together to support each other, to challenge each other, and to serve as resources. Your Prosperity Partners can be like-minded businesspeople, investors, family members, friends, and former colleagues. All that is required is that you gather to support each other collectively in pursuing your individual goals.

One challenge you'll face as you're moving forward to create something vitally important to you is that you'll receive all kinds of feedback, some of it contradictory. It's vital to be able to listen to what people have to say but not allow anyone to derail you. Not all people are helpful, even if most of them are well intended.

The Crab Mentality

As we said, most people mean well, but that doesn't mean some of them aren't toxic. Every once in a while, we hear from students who have started on their prosperity journey but find that their plans are being criticized, questioned, or belittled by a loved one or close friend. The more intimate the relationship, it seems, the more personal the challenge. We call this dynamic the "crab mentality."

Have you ever seen a large pot full of live crabs? Typically what happens is one particularly ambitious or intelligent crab tries to escape by grabbing the lid and slowly pulling its way out of the pot. Other crabs could take its example and try to do the same, but something else happens instead. Before the crab can get very far, the other crabs pull it back. The human analogy is that of a group attempting to pull back any member who aspires to or achieves success beyond the others. Frequently, the community asserts a false sense of solidarity: "What's the matter? Do you think you're too good for us?"

It's not hard to see what's happening. After all, if you move forward with passion and commitment, others struggling with their situations will have one less excuse for not doing the same. It's much easier to pull you back than to face the humiliation of being left behind. What all these people have in common is that they are thinking more about themselves than about you. As far as your Prosperity Path is concerned, whatever anyone says, they are in the wrong if they do not take into account who you really are, what you care about deeply, and what you know to be true about yourself. The crab mentality is thankfully rare, but it does happen, so you should be prepared for it.

TAKE PROFOUND ACTION

Prosperity Steps

Profound Action is not just any action. By Profound Action, we mean action that has three elements. First, it is supportive of the decision. Second, it is aligned with your core values and passions. And third, it is consistent with your *why*.

Complete this Prosperity Step online at www.prosperbook.com/PS6.

Profound Action Tips

- Commit to continuous action
- Say "yes" to "no"
- Move quickly
- Have faith in yourself
- Have the courage to stick to your decision
- Don't turn back
- Find Prosperity Partners
- Watch for the crab mentality

Profound Action Questions

1. What one specific action would have the greatest impact on my succeeding in my goals?
2. What is the one action that I most need to take today?
3. What do I feel inspired and ready to do now?
4. What are the negotiable and non-negotiable aspects of my action plan?

CHAPTER 7

PROSPERITY
IN MOTION

The biggest mistake people make in life is not trying
to make a living at doing what they most enjoy.

—Malcolm Forbes

In this final chapter, we will show you how Rebecca Miller did it. In this case history, we will walk you through all of the Six Prosperity Practices that Rebecca considered. This case history reproduces all the worksheets that she was asked to complete and provides her responses. Our hope is that by tracking Rebecca's progress through this case history, you will have a better understanding of how the steps fit together and how they are used in a typical coaching engagement.

By following one student's process from beginning to end, we hope you will better appreciate the power of the Six Prosperity Practices and how they fit together. Chapter 5 presented the Prosperity Blueprint of one student, but it doesn't show you how he got there. In this chapter, we show how a student goes step by step through the Six Prosperity Practices.

Please note that for this case history, we have selected a student on an entrepreneurial path to find her Prosperity Zone. We could have focused on a student whose preference was to work within his or her organization, or a student on a journey of personal growth. We also have had hundreds of students who have wanted new careers, such as in personal finance or currency exchange trading, who we could have profiled in this chapter. We chose this particular case as the one that best allows us to demonstrate, as fully as possible, how the Six Prosperity Practices fit together in a coordinated plan.

INTRODUCING REBECCA MILLER

Rebecca Miller, age 38, lives in Milwaukee with her husband, Bud, and two children, April, age 8, and David, age 6. Rebecca has a bachelor's degree in business administration. Before she started her family, she worked as the marketing director of a health spa. She quit when the stress of working a full-time job and taking care of her family started to take a toll on her health. Her husband Bud works in construction. He makes a good living when he works, but the income fluctuates with the season, and the job is not secure. The monthly income of the Miller household ranges from $3,000 to $5,000, and most months little or nothing is usually left over for savings.

Rebecca came to us because she wanted to contribute more to the economic well-being of her family by doing something that would fulfill her. She does not want to go back to working as a low-level employee. Rebecca's goal is to start an Internet-based business that she can operate from her home on her own schedule. Moreover, she wants to start a business that she can enjoy because she's working with something that interests her. The income from the business should pave the way to prosperity for the Miller family.

By the way, we like to work with people like Rebecca who have some idea about what they want and how they want to achieve it.

Every coach will tell you that people who start with a direction—
even if that direction subsequently changes—have a better chance
of success than those who come in with an "I'll do whatever"
attitude.

Quentin, one of our best certified coaches, was assigned to assist
Rebecca. The first thing Quentin did was to ask her a number of
questions and listen carefully to the answers. Here's what he asked
and what she told him. Normally, this exchange involves conversation and written questionnaires.

Quentin *How do you feel about your present situation in life?*

Rebecca *I feel like I can do more and want to contribute to the family's
income. I'm stressed out about making sure that all the bills are paid
and that my family is taken care of. I've worked very hard to get where
we are now, and with the cost of everything going up, I'm afraid that I
won't be able to keep up. We've been living paycheck to paycheck off
my husband's income. We have a nest egg, but I don't want to see that
disappear with my fickle business right now.*

Quentin *Please list three results you are committed to achieving over
the next ninety days.*

Rebecca *(1) Finally decide on what idea or product I want to market
(2) Get a Web site up and running. (3) Make my first dollar on the
Internet.*

Quentin *Why do you feel these goals are most important?*

Rebecca *I need to get past the initial roadblock of not knowing what
my business will be about, so that's the first thing I feel I need to decide.
I also know that a great Web site is integral to every Internet-based
business. I don't have a business without a Web site. And I know myself.
Nothing will probably get me as psyched as my first sale. A good first
sale will keep me motivated for months.*

Quentin *What has stopped you from accomplishing these results in the past?*

Rebecca *Working my forty-hour-a-week job and then coming home and taking care of my kids just left me too exhausted. I am overwhelmed with all of the information out there about how to start a Web-based business. I'm not confident that the product I will choose to sell will make money for me. Then there's my lack of knowledge, which is fixable, but is nevertheless present. That's why I feel I need guidance to get started.*

Quentin *What do you consider your four biggest accomplishments in life?*

Rebecca *A happy marriage with two beautiful children. Graduating from college with a degree and landing a good job after college in my field of study. Working my way up from marketing intern at a day spa to the marketing director position. Buying our first house.*

Quentin *When you later look back on your life, what do you want to have accomplished in this lifetime?*

(*Note:* Quentin is asking for Rebecca's Polaris Point here.)

Rebecca *Be successful in all of my relationships, have a successful business, know that I did everything I could to achieve my goals, donate to charity, have prosperity—not just in money terms, but in all aspects of my life. That means having the freedom to travel, to help others, and to know that I have added value to all my relationships. I want to be able to enjoy life with my husband and children instead of working and worrying all the time. I want to be debt-free, own my house free and clear, and have a profitable business.*

Quentin *What habits do you believe you need to drop, change, or adopt to achieve your goals?*

Rebecca *The habits I need to drop are fear of failure, procrastination, and self-doubt. The habits I need to adopt are impeccable goal setting, prioritizing, and time management.*

Quentin *What motivates or inspires you the most? Why are those things important to you?*

Rebecca *My family. They give me purpose in life. Without them, I would be just another person looking for something to live for. Right now, the biggest thing weighing on me is not having free time to do what I want when I want. So doing something that could give me more freedom is really motivating. Not living paycheck to paycheck is motivating so that I can feel like I am contributing to the household; having the money to travel to experience new things and cultures.*

Quentin *We want to educate you in the most effective and personalized way possible. Describe your preferred learning style.*

Rebecca *When given a task, I am very good at getting it done. However, I tend to lack the imagination and skills to take initiative to do things on my own. So I would do very well with things being outlined for me. I am also a very visual learner. I like to see things and how they fit together before I do them on my own.*

I have spent a lot of time in school, and I learn best from hands-on and discussion. I like to bounce ideas back and forth person to person, because there is more to communication than just words.

Quentin *Is there anything else you want to share that might help your coach support you?*

Rebecca *I feel like I can't get past the obstacle of finding that perfect idea or product. I understand the whole market research thing, but I am very uncertain about being able to take it to the next level. Guidance as far as that goes would be great. When I feel overwhelmed, I have a tendency to go underground for a day or two. It is my way of taking a break, getting myself together and tackling whatever needs to be done. I know that habit doesn't serve me well.*

Quentin *How will you determine the effectiveness of your one-on-one coaching program?*

Rebecca *If I am achieving my weekly goals and seeing tangible progress, then that would be effective for me. I would also need to see a financial benefit to consider this program a success. This may be shallow,
but money talks. If I am able to work from home, pay the bills, travel
when and where I want, then that will be the determining factor as far
as effectiveness of coaching.*

Quentin *What major changes do you believe you need to make in order to achieve success through this program?*

Rebecca *Develop a more positive mind-set, time management, be
very open-minded. Work on not procrastinating.*

WORKING THE PRACTICES

At this point, let's follow Rebecca as she goes through the Six
Prosperity Practices that the previous chapters discussed. Note
the responses she gives to the same worksheets we invited you
to complete at the end of Chapters 1 through 6. The goal is for
the student to meet his or her prosperity desires and to follow his
or her Polaris Point—not to check off boxes on a coaching work-
sheet.

Let's review the Six Prosperity Practices before we get into Rebecca Miller's responses.

Practice 1. Locate Your Polaris Point

Practice 2. Live in Your Prosperity Zone

Practice 3. Earn from Your Core

Practice 4. Start with What You Already Have

Practice 5. Commit to Your Prosperity Path

Practice 6: Take Profound Action

Practice 1. Rebecca Locates Her Polaris Point. This is how Rebecca Miller created her list in the first step of the Prosperity Steps in Chapter 1. Her next step is to go through a process of elimination to identify, first, her top ten things she values most, and second, her top three. She starts by brainstorming a list and selecting her top ten that seem most significant to her by putting a single line through everything else. In the third step, Rebecca double strikes until only three remain.

What Rebecca Values Most

Happiness	~~Innovation~~	~~Chic and Trendy~~
~~Openness~~	~~Positive~~	~~Wardrobe~~
~~Cabin on the~~	~~Organized~~	~~Determined~~
~~Lake~~	~~Honesty~~	~~Six Figure Annual Salary~~
~~Doing Good~~	~~Passion~~	~~Wealth~~
~~Loyalty~~	~~Floor Seats to~~	~~Good Citizen~~
Relationships	~~Lakers~~	~~Frugal~~
~~Frequent Travel~~	~~Helpful~~	Integrity
~~Purpose~~	~~Loving~~	~~Clean~~
~~Faith~~	~~Quality~~	~~Self-respect~~
~~Freedom~~	~~Family Time~~	~~Luxury Car~~

Now, with respect to her top three attributes—happiness, relationships, and integrity—Rebecca gives short responses to the following questions.

1. What do your selections have in common?

   All centered on high-quality relationships.

2. Does the way you earn your income today align with the things most important to you?

   Yes. Even though I could earn an income without integrity, I wouldn't want to.

3. What does the list say about what you are expecting from yourself?

Work-life balance. Continue being a people person, and use inter-personal relationship building as a strength and asset.

4. How would your life and career be different if you consistently focused on those things you value most?

I would have fun doing something that resonates with me and engages my passions and talents.

5. Does this list reflect the way you actually conduct your life?

Yes, I'm all about making something truly mine.

Rebecca's Polaris Point Statement

Rebecca starts by simply listing her three highest attributes.

My Polaris Point includes happiness, integrity, and relationships.

Then she writes out a framing statement of her Polaris Point, embracing those three values, by starting the statement with the words "I promise to guide every aspect of my life by . . ."

I promise to guide every aspect of my life by unwavering loyalty to my most deeply held values of integrity and relationships. A life anchored in these qualities will result in happiness based on earning from my core and deepest priorities. These values will be guiding, stationary beacons to my life through meandering trials and questions. The framework for my answers will be rooted in these core values.

Practice 2. Rebecca Finds Her Prosperity Zone. Rebecca's Prosperity Zone is the place where what she loves to do more than anything in the whole world also makes her money. She is truly living her best life when what makes her money makes her and other people happy—when work doesn't seem like work at all. She occupies the Prosperity Zone when she is able to balance her desire for happiness with what she earns and how she earns it.

Next, Rebecca responds to the questions in the Prosperity Steps section of Chapter 2. How many of these questions can she honestly answer "yes" to?

1. Is there alignment between how you are earning a living and your core?

   Yes.

2. Are your "stretch goals" based on the confidence that comes from focusing on what you have instead of desperation over what you lack?

   Yes.

3. Are you making steady progress in growing your income so that you can fund your lifestyle and still have something left over to save? Invest? Give away?

   Yes, Yes, Yes.

4. Are you happy because your happiness corresponds with your values, talents, and passions?

   Yes.

5. Do you have systems or networks in place to support you?

   Working on it. Growing it everyday.

6. Do you celebrate the victories, big and small, as you fix your sights on your Polaris Point?

   Yes.

7. Are you giving chunks of your prosperity away to create value and better the lives of others?

Yes, although I wish it to grow over time.

Money

1. Is your financial outlook positive?

Yes.

2. Do you have excess after all of your financial obligations are met?

Yes, not much, but yes.

3. Do you enjoy what you do for income?

Yes.

4. Do you feel like your income is aligned with your passion?

Yes.

5. Are you on track to make more money this year than last year?

Yes.

6. Do you feel like you are thriving? (Or just surviving?)

Thriving.

Happiness

1. Are you generally happy with your current place in life and where you are heading?

Not always, but I'm working on it.

2. Do you know where you are heading?

Yes.

3. Do you feel like you are moving forward? (Or backward/ stagnant?)

Yes, forward!

4. Are you happy about the different facets of your life? (Personal, Family, Career, Physical, and Financial?)

All yes.

5. Do you have a positive personal image and live with your own "personal vibe"?

It's sometimes a struggle to stay "up," but that's my goal.

6. Are you able to be happy for others when they experience success?

That's easy. Yes.

Sustainability

1. Do you feel like you are growing personally, professionally, and financially?

Yes.

2. Are you able to share and give away some of your prosperity?

Not much yet, but I give what I can.

3. Are you joyfully and deliberately celebrating life and all your victories?

Yes.

4. Do you have a long-term plan to grow your current happiness and wealth?

Yes.

5. Have you diversified your income sources?

Still need to work on this part.

6. Do you evaluate your Polaris Point often and make proper adjustments to your course?

Yes.

Based on her responses to these questions, Rebecca is gratified by how much she has accomplished. After a period of gratified reflection, she realizes which areas require further development. She is confident that she is on a sound path to live in her Prosperity Zone.

Practice 3. Rebecca Earns from Her Core. Rebecca feels a little overwhelmed at the task in front of her. She is afraid of all the competition out there, and she doesn't really know how she will distinguish herself from the rest. She knows that in marketing you need to have a brand, and she is struggling to find her voice in the marketplace. She feels like she is a jack of all trades but a master of none. She is struggling to find out how her passions will translate into a return on investment. She hears her parents' advice echoing in her mind—"Chose something you love to do, and you'll never work a day in your life"—yet also sees her friends who majored in things they liked in college but can't find a job, or who are doing something totally outside of their degree areas. She is excited about the coaching sessions teaching her how to monetize her core.

At this point, Rebecca transfers her three top Polaris Point priorities to complete the Polaris Point statement.

Polaris Point Priority I	Polaris Point Priority 2	Polaris Point Priority 3
Happiness	Relationships	Integrity

My Polaris Point Statement

I promise to guide every aspect of my life by unwavering loyalty to my most deeply held values of integrity and relationships. A life anchored in these qualities will result in happiness based on earning from my core and deepest priorities. These values will be guiding, stationary beacons to my life through meandering trials and questions. The framework for my answers will be rooted in these core values.

Next, she provides answers to the following questions:

1. What is your definition of your core in thirty words or less?

   Aligning core values into a business model servicing the health spa and massage niche. Preeminence, uniqueness, value, and quality are the hallmarks of our products and services.

2. Name five enterprises/businesses aligned with your passion and core. What are their business models? Which ones offer the most value or reward?

   Johnston Health Services

   Gardner Massage

   Holistic Health Spa

   Kendrick School of Massage

3. How can I be the best at doing this? What will make me different, better, and special? What will be my personal vibe?

   I will sell products directly on my site to the spas and new massage therapists—these products would include but not be limited to massage tables, massage chairs, high-end oils, organic towels and robes, and organic salon-quality skin-care products. In phase 2, I would start a B-C (Business to Consumer) Web site which will offer various levels of gift baskets for the public and include a blog where I review products, services, and businesses, specifically in the spa industry.

4. How will you be compensated? What is your yardstick to measure success?

My mark-up is where my profit comes from. In my B-B (Business to Business) Web site, I will have products that I drop-ship to my customers. This allows me to bring buyers and manufacturers together without any out-of-pocket cost. I will be the online storefront for the products. It's what I'll earn for locating manufacturers—and even some "green, environmentally friendly" manufacturers—and making their products available for spas and for individual buyers. I'll make the site attractive and relevant by expanding it into an online community where spa owners and massage therapists can exchange ideas about how to care for customers and the like.

I will measure my success by profits and revenue. As the business grows, my yardstick will be a reduction in fear and worry about our finances, my contribution to the family income, our growing nest egg, and more freedom to be a family and travel together. I want to give my children opportunities I never had. I would like to create a tradition for Christmas trips and family time. My husband and I see the value of education. I would like to begin a college savings fund for my children.

Practice 4. Rebecca Starts with What She Already Has. Having established a trusting relationship with Rebecca, Quentin is ready to start the process. Many of his questions have already started Rebecca thinking about the assets she has to work with. Like many people just starting the coaching process, Rebecca has emphasized the deficits (ignorance, procrastination, self-doubt) that she is bringing to the table. Quentin tells her that this is normal—most of the critical feedback we get from life focuses on our supposed deficits. Coaching is different in that it focuses instead on strengths and assets. As for those supposed deficits, coaching reframes those as opportunities for growth. The goal of the first step is to really drill down and work through a series of exercises to get Rebecca to become aware of her many assets.

Some of Rebecca's frustrations emerge at this first step. At first, Rebecca believes that she has no unique quality to her life, and that makes choosing a product difficult. She considers herself to have a fairly normal life and average experiences, certainly nothing unique that she could leverage. She is frustrated that she will end up with a "me-too" company selling a "me-too" product.

Rebecca is truly excited about the prospect of making money online. At the same time, she is scared because she has never been a business owner. She has only the slightest idea of what a limited liability corporation (LLC) is and no idea how to set one up. She has always worked for someone else, and she has been the technician, never the thought leader or entrepreneur. Quentin understands that Rebecca is scared about what she doesn't know, but he is also aware of how curious she is. Quentin reminds Rebecca that she doesn't have to know everything to start making decisions. Nor does she need to do everything by herself. The first thing Rebecca needs, Quentin tells her, is to decide on what her core is as the basis for her product and business.

Rebecca starts this section by noting all that she is grateful for.

I am most grateful for my health, my beautiful children, my loving/supportive husband, my immediate and extended family who are willing to help us with our children, and my abundant world, every freedom I've enjoyed, and the desire and ability to achieve something significant in my life.

I feel my life has been blessed in the last ninety days because of my husband's job, my family's good health, my oldest daughter's creativity and continual ability to surprise me with what she knows and absorbs, my son's natural ability with technology, the realization of the support of parents and siblings, the new lessons and joys of parenthood every day brings, the opportunity to be a stay-at-home mom, the patience and understanding for the trade-offs of my decision to be at home, our volunteering at our local church, weekend picnics with the kids, and getting a tax refund.

Rebecca's Completed Asset Inventory

Asset Inventory		
Unique Life Experiences and Expertise	Unique Abilities, Talents, and Passions	Personal Contacts, Networks, and Business Connections
Being a mom of two children. Stay-at-home mom.	*Kids/children/ parenting.*	*Neighborhood play-group.*
BS in marketing communications.	*Health trends, health and wellness.*	*MLM vitamin distributors (parents).*
High school newspaper editor.	*Traveling out of the country.*	*Volunteer at a local music class that my daughter attends.*
Marketing director at a day spa for three years. Organic products.	*Ultra-health conscious.*	*Neighborhood Watch.*
Bargain hunter.	*Reading and writing.*	*Local triathlon club.*

Completed half and full marathon. Training for marathons and sprint triathlons.	Competition. I am a very driven individual.	Member of the American Marketing Association.
Competitive swimmer in high school and college. College injury ended my competitive swimming career. Had twelve months of physical therapy for my injury.	Organic, and natural, and homeopathic remedies.	Worked at a day spa for three years and still have connections there.
Vitamins and health.	Creative/crafts.	Physical therapists.
Computer savvy.	Helping friends and family, volunteering.	Yoga class.
	Organizing/planning.	Lamaze class instructor.
	Dedicated and consistent blogger.	Sister is a soon-to-be massage therapist graduate.

Practice 5. Rebecca Commits to Her Prosperity Path. Rebecca needs to see the big picture, all of its parts, and understand how they all fit together. She is confused. She sees where she is right now and the end of the game, but she doesn't quite understand how she will get from point A to point B. She feels as though the business is coming together. She has had her logo designed, and this was a huge boost for her. She feels as though she is in business now and that she can show someone she is in business. She makes business cards, and

she and her husband celebrate. She then fills out the mind map to get a hold of all the moving parts of the system. She has already started on the first items of her business.

My Polaris Point

I promise to guide every aspect of my life by unwavering loyalty to my most deeply held values of integrity and relationships. A life anchored in these qualities will result in happiness based on earning from my core and deepest priorities. These values will be guiding, stationary beacons to my life through meandering trials and questions. The framework for my life's answers will be rooted in these core values.

Earn from My Core

Aligning core values into a business model servicing the health spa and massage niche. Preeminence, uniqueness, value, and quality are the hallmarks of our products and services.

Start with What I Already Have

Through my experience as a marketing director in the spa and massage industries, I am uniquely positioned to provide solutions to the needs and problems of this arena. With a passion for health, and a firsthand knowledge of the healing potential of massage therapy, I will create a world-class Web site servicing small-business day spas and burgeoning massage therapists.

Prosperity Path Questions

1. What problem am I trying to solve?

   So many spas and massage therapists are great at what they do (technicians), but lack the understanding (how), skill (what), time, and patience to identify and locate the best-quality massage and spa products at the best possible prices.

2. What is it that I am selling or offering?

A relationship with a spa/masseuse product supplier who will grow with the needs of their business.

3. What is my distribution channel?

My online Web site.

4. How am I going to let people know what I am offering?

By Web site, newsletters, strategic partnerships, social media, word of mouth, and direct through massage therapy schools.

5. Who is my target customer?

Small day spas (five to ten employees) and new massage therapists.

6. How much are people willing to pay for a solution to this problem?

A premium for outstanding service, telephone consultations on exactly the product lines they need, ultra quick shipping, with our 110 percent guarantee.

7. What offers similar to mine are already available?

Other sites have phone assistance for shopping on their site, but they are typically outsourced telemarketing floors. Our staff will be massage/spa industry veterans with a vast array of experience to know how to broaden offerings and product lines.

8. What makes my offer better, unique, special?

Guarantee on products, information on our site regarding choosing the right product, our customer service, and the quality/experience of the reps helping people on the site.

9. How will I articulate my solution to the customers?

We will have a "live chat with an expert" box on every page. The USP will permeate every piece of marketing material we have, along with being included in every communication point (e-mail signatures, slogan, business cards, etc.).

Reasons Why I Want Prosperity

College fund for the kids.

Financial security. (I want to stop dipping into the nest egg and save for retirement.)

Personal satisfaction. (I enjoyed being in the workforce, and I want to continue to contribute to the family's income.)

Lifestyle. (I love traveling. I have a lot of exotic locations on my bucket list. I want to take my children to new places and have them experience new things, cultures, and people. I don't want to live my life vicariously through Google Earth or books.)

Charitable giving. (I'd love to start my own nonprofit one day.)

Prosperity Visualization

1. Where do you now live?

   We have paid off our home and have rented it out. We have recently purchased a 4,500 sq. ft. rambler with a finished basement in a gated community twenty minutes across town. It's our dream home. We drive through this part of town a lot on Sunday drives with the family. There is a fantastic park where the kids love to play. The best part of the school district is that it has some of the highest marks in the state. My kids will love it. It is about fifteen minutes closer for my husband's commute so he can run home for lunch, or we can drop by and visit. The best part was when we bought it: we paid cash. I love not having a mortgage payment.

2. What kind of car do you drive?

   We've upgraded from the ten-year-old minivan and are now driving a black Cadillac Escalade. The kids love it because it has the full enter-

tainment package. *My husband loves it because he put on 22-inch chrome rims. I love it because it has a backup camera and leather interior. It has the new car smell that makes it worth every cent.*

3. How are you supporting yourself?

The Web sites are doing fabulously well. My husband still works, but it's because he likes to. I am contributing to the family income, our nest egg, and my children's future. I have actually taken up learning more about online investing in the stock market. By trading, I'm learning financial management and even producing an extra source of income.

4. How much are you earning?

The business is now grossing $250,000 a year. Out of that I draw a salary that is twice what I made as an employee.

5. What are the hobbies you actively pursue?

I have taken up guitar and golf, while also dabbling in the stock market. I have gotten back to swimming in the evenings.

6. Where was the last place you took a two-week vacation?

We spent a week on Oahu and then a week on Kauai. We took a helicopter ride around the island that the kids still talk about. The black sand beaches and the hiking were amazing. I have never seen a sunset that vibrant. I can still smell the fragrance of the Puakenikeni tree next to our condo.

Prosperity Goals

Today: *Call three new suppliers.*

Tomorrow: *Add one new product category to my site with five new products.*

Next week: *Write three compelling blog posts.*

Next month: *Register domain name for my new site and hire a designer to develop new off-shoot brand.*

Next year: *Double current revenue from new site while diversifying product line through spa reviews and gift baskets. New B-C site will also have subscriber list of 5,000 and a modest following on Facebook and Twitter.*

The year after: *Both sites are ranked extremely well in all major search engines for multiple keyword phrases. We have over 1,000 unique visitors to both sites each day, and 10 percent of the sites' income comes from advertising and sponsorships.*

Three years from now: *I am working in the business about 25 percent of the time, and I have turned over the day-to-day operations to my sister. We have ten employees now processing orders, creating content, and managing relationships with vendors and suppliers. We take vacations three times a year and have made it a family tradition to take the grandparents on a Christmas vacation with us.*

Five years from now: *The business is growing, and over 50 percent of clientele are from word-of-mouth marketing. We have successfully launched our "refer a friend" loyalty program. We have won several best-in-class industry awards for our customer service. Service levels and answer rates for both of our sites are our hallmark. Our nestegg is growing each month. I realize how far I've come personally and professionally.*

Ten years from now: *We take the entire company of ten employees on a three-day cruise in celebration of our best year in terms of top-line revenue. We have over 12,000 unique visitors to the sites daily, with 90 percent organic traffic coming from natural rankings, and have a Google page rank of 7. Our database is massive now at over 350,000 subscribers, and we invest in a more robust CRM system to maintain customer intimacy. We've diversified the business income streams to include marketing/branding packages for massage therapists and spas, paid advertising, e-mail marketing, affiliate programs, drop-shipping, eBay sales, and manufacturing our own product line. This year marks the opening of our own corporate 3,000 sq. ft. office space to an adjoining local spa. We've partnered with multiple massage therapy schools to provide private-label equipment for their students and therapists.*

Prosperity Agreement

I, *Rebecca Miller*, hereby commit to the achievement of my Prosperity Path. I agree to set strong boundaries, to "show up" and "be present." I understand that I need to hold myself accountable for my actions because "if it's to be, it's up to me." I agree to commit at least 5 to 10 hours per week to developing my future prosperity. I will pledge to take action in creating the life I truly want and to uphold the values I stand for. I promise to recognize the abundance I already have while achieving my goals along my Prosperity Path. I understand that with the expectation of new results in my life comes an expectation of new actions. I commit fully to these required actions in the fulfillment of my goals.

Rebecca Miller

Practice 6. Rebecca Takes Profound Action. Rebecca is now ready to assemble all the pieces of the puzzle. She feels that she has turned all of the pieces of the business over in her mind so that she now understands not only how all the pieces operate individually but in coordination. Rebecca now starts to put the steps into action following an established time-line. Working the Prosperity Practices, she outlines the tasks and steps, owners, and dates of completion. She understands the need for an exact order in doing things correctly and thoroughly. Her Web site is almost complete, with descriptions of the products; the e-commerce steps are nearly complete. She has worked her network and made significant new contacts.

This process has not been without frustration. Networking is often the most taxing part of the process because it is the most unpredictable part. She is also learning every day. In coaching sessions, Rebecca reviews her networking initiatives and concludes that on occasion she has put considerable resources into building relationships with people who are not really the decision makers or gatekeepers that success requires. Working with Quentin, she designates some set milestones that she feels are significant to her business and her coaching progress: (1) business setup, (2) Web site launched, and (3) first sale online.

Here's how Rebecca answered the Profound Action questions.

1. What one specific action would have the greatest impact on my succeeding in my goals?

   I need to make time to grow my business by creating a schedule. Life seems to fill up with things to do—kids, family, errands, music lessons, carpool, etc. I need to schedule time specifically for my business. Most people who go to work have a schedule and are paid to show up to work. I need to discipline myself to keep to a schedule of five to ten hours a week.

   I need to do more of what makes me more, and less of what makes me less. One specific thing that I can do is blog on my site more often. I often get behind and end up trying to write four postings in a single day. Readers like consistency, and they like fresh content. I notice that when I wait to "batch blog" the content seems contrived and less genuine. I commit to posting on Monday, Wednesday, and Friday. Blogging has consistently proven to be great for my site's search engine optimization, and I have made contacts with suppliers and customers through some of my previous postings.

2. What is the one action that I most need to take today?

   I need to prioritize my tasks and make a "not to do" list. I've noticed that I really get sidetracked with starting and stopping work on my site because of the e-mails and distractions. I need to focus on the priorities of working: my goal is to call five potential suppliers to develop my gift basket product line and to add at least one of them to my site this week.

I also need to formalize my "spa review" critique sheet. In order for me to really provide consistent ratings and reviews, I need to grade all the spas the exact same way. This sheet will be critical so that anyone on my staff can use the same rating system to make the reviews compare apples with apples.

3. What do I feel inspired and ready to do now?

I am going to talk with my sister Chelsea about her joining my business. I want to make sure that orders get processed in a timely manner, and quite frankly I am more passionate about the spa reviews and the B-C side. I want to launch the new arm of the business within the next thirty to forty-five days. This is going to be awesome!

4. What are the negotiable and non-negotiable aspects of my action plan?

With my sister assisting me and with the current success of my site, I can grow the new site at my leisure. I know that this will require a rigid, set schedule since a huge part of the growth will be blogging. I also realize that I will have to really put forth my personal "brand." I will have to develop myself and establish myself as an authority on a lot of the social media sites.

I'd like to expand my presence and reputation online from just the business to being known in my space personally. The negotiable parts of this plan are (1) my personal involvement with the primary Web site (my sister is more than capable of running it), and (2) how quickly I grow the review side of the new site. The non-negotiable parts are (1) blogging frequency, (2) social media exposure, (3) finding suppliers for the new site, and (4) work-life balance. I don't want to lose myself in my work because I originally started this whole business so that I would have more financial ability to spend time with my family doing what I wanted to do. I made a decision to stay home with the kids. I don't want to lose focus on that decision.

Renewing Prosperity

Rebecca now takes a moment to consider her progress. Her coach advocates celebrating along the path, not just at the end. She writes him an e-mail about her progress so far, noting what she did when she hit the first three milestones. She mentions that she had two additional occasions for celebration with her husband and family: (1) when her logo design was completed and (2) when she earned her first $1,000—the family took a trip.

When Rebecca returned from celebrating making her first $1,000, she had a flood of mixed emotions because she was still on a high from the vacation that her business had paid for—essentially, the first fruits of a change in her lifestyle—while also feeling sluggish about putting more effort and focus into growing and maintaining her business. Rebecca is excited about her progress, yet she is keen to ensure that the business isn't taking her away from the family she finds so important.

In her personal life, Rebecca is renewing her prosperity through several areas. The evidence for this is clear not only to herself but also to her friends and family, who notice that Rebecca is more centered and content. Here's why Rebecca is proud:

- She has established a college fund for her children.
- She's contributing to an emergency fund of her own, which is growing.
- She has more time to spend with her family.
- She has more opportunity to volunteer at the music class her daughter attends.
- She has time to focus on the networking and marketing side of her business, including the aspects of the business, such as blogging, that she enjoys.

- She's defined her life as an independent businesswoman, independent of her identity as a wife and mother.
- She's strengthened her relationship with her husband because she is now, like Bud, contributing her share to the family income.

Rebecca has worked hard to get to this point. She's put her focus on what she has instead of what she doesn't have. She's located her Polaris Point. She's learned how to earn from her core. She's named her Prosperity Path and claimed it. She's taken Profound Action, and it has paid off. Here she is at the gates of the Prosperity Zone. Congratulations Rebecca! She deserves to acknowledge her having made her dream into reality.

CONCLUSION

Renew Your Prosperity

We are kept from our goal not by obstacles, but a clear path to a lesser goal.

—Robert Brault

Prosperity is not a recreational activity but a lifestyle that you have to choose and renew. We hope you have seen the power of the Six Prosperity Practices and how they can be a basis for meaningful change in creating the life you want.

We call this renewing your prosperity, and there are three ways to do so.

1. Retake the Prosperity Assessment.
2. Cycle through the Six Prosperity Practices more than once.
3. Give to others.

RETAKE THE PROSPERITY ASSESSMENT

Our first request of you was for you to take the Prosperity Assessment and study your results. Now we ask you to go to www.prosper book.com/assessment and take it again. Notice the differences in your results. What about the 360-degree assessment? Have those results changed? What attributes of prosperity have you more fully developed? What do you think that means? What assumptions about prosperity did you challenge?

What do these changes mean to you? The Assessment hasn't changed. If the results are different, it's because of a change in you.

Think of the Prosperity Assessment like your blood pressure, which you monitor to determine your cardiovascular health. Just as you check your blood pressure many times over the course of a year, we recommend you do the same with the health of your levels of prosperity. The Prosperity Assessment does just that by giving you information that helps you reinforce positive behaviors and correct any bad habits that occasionally slip in. Each set of results allows you to assess where you are in your journey to prosperity and make adjustments to get you to your Polaris Point faster.

Our prosperity journeys are never complete because people are always changing. We are always cycling back to the beginning to find out just where it is we are heading. There are always insights to be had by repeating and revaluating the Prosperity Assessment.

CYCLE THROUGH THE SIX PROSPERITY PRACTICES MORE THAN ONCE

If you went through the Six Prosperity Practices and completed all the Prosperity Steps, congratulations! We are confident you are now better prepared to make the decisions and take the actions that will improve your life. But guess what? The quest for prosperity is never finished.

Going through the Six Prosperity Practices and seeing the added benefits to your life are a great start. But it's just that—a start to a process that repeats, with each repetition adding to your prosperity.

We regard the Six Prosperity Practices not so much as a list of items to strike off your to-do list, but more as milestones on a never-ending cycle.

We promise you that when you repeat the cycle, the ground you cover will be very different because you will be different and your circumstances will have changed. For example, when you come to the third practice (Earn from Your Core), the experience will be very different because by this time you may have taken action on a new venture or new career. You will have enhanced skills and perspectives. We see the Six Prosperity Practices as a totally connected, continuous cycle.

As we indicated previously, this would be a good time to retake the Prosperity Assessment. Remember you can take it an unlimited number of times.

Just as a rough rock rolling down a moving river becomes smoother with every rotation, you will become more and more prosperous with every rotation of the Six Prosperity Practices. It is a cycle that gives you greater depth of perspective. You will see the problems and their solutions with new eyes.

We ask you to renew your prosperity by making these practices an ongoing process in your life.

GIVE PROSPERITY TO OTHERS

You know you are really living in the Prosperity Zone when your passion shifts from accumulating to giving. It's no coincidence that the most prosperous people in the world have committed to giving the bulk of their wealth away.

The Prosperity Assessment that we have made available to you at no cost is just one expression of our commitment to giving. The assessment is free. We encourage you to take it as often as you want. Feel free to share it with as many friends and associates as you can.

We believe that everyone walks around with an invisible prosperity pail. We all have one, and it is always with us. Sometimes the pail is overflowing, and sometimes it is drained. It's natural to want a pail that is full rather than one that is empty—the fuller, the better. How we keep our pails full is to live in a way that is consistent with our Polaris Point.

However, having our pails full to the brim is not the ultimate victory. Our pails can be enlarged. The secret? Fill up the prosperity buckets of other people. How do we do this? It's unfortunate that many people are going through life with a low prosperity level. By helping them identify and live their potential of a prosperous life, their buckets fill up. When you help them understand that there is a Prosperity Zone where they can turn their prosperity level to a high setting, you are filling their pail. The magic is that your own pail will not only fill up accordingly but will expand.

The actions we take in life fill some containers and empty others. We don't pretend to understand that mystery, but this we do know: the story of our lives is the interplay of the dipper and the pail, and over that interplay we do have control. We always have a choice to be a prosperity taker or a giver. The lesson we have learned is that the best way we can fill our own pails and help them grow is by filling someone else's.

REFERENCES

Baum, Herb, and Tammy Kling. *The Transparent Leader: How to Build a Great Company through Straight Talk, Openness, and Accountability.* New York: HarperCollins, 2004.

Brickman, P., D. Coates, and R. Janoff-Bulman. "Lottery Winners and Accident Victims: Is Happiness Relative?" *Journal of Personality and Social Psychology* 36, no. 8 (August 1978): 917–927.

Christensen, Clayton M. "How Will You Measure Your Life?" *Harvard Business Review,* July–August 2010. Available at http://hbr.org/2010/07/how-will-you-measure-your-life/ar/1.

Firebaugh, Glenn, and Laura Tach. "Income and Happiness in the United States." Paper presented at the annual meeting of the American Sociological Association, Philadelphia, PA, August 12, 2005. Available at http://www.allacademic.com/meta/p18167_index.html.

Gladwell, Malcolm. *Outliers: The Story of Success.* New York: Little, Brown, 2008.

Goodrich, Laura. *Seeing Red Cars: Driving Yourself, Your Team, and Your Organization to a Positive Future*. San Francisco: Berrett-Koehler, 2011.

Kent, Linda Tarr. "What Is Hedonic Treadmill?" Available at http://www.livestrong.com/article/386749-what-is-hedonic -treadmill/#ixzz1NEhYQsV0.

Reitman, Jason, Walter Kirn, and Sheldon Turner. *Up in the Air*, DVD. Directed by Jason Reitman. Hollywood: Paramount Home Entertainment, 2010.

Shermer, Michael. "It Doesn't Add Up: Why People Believe Weird Things About Money." *Los Angeles Times*, January 13, 2008. Available at http://articles.latimes.com/2008/jan/13/opinion/op-schermer13.

Souman, Jan L., Ilja Frissen, Manish N. Sreenivasa, and Marc O. Ernst. "Walking Straight into Circles." *Current Biology* 19, no. 18 (2009): 1538–1542.

ACKNOWLEDGMENTS

It would be inaccurate to say that this book was written by any one person, or even by two. This book is a product of so many people giving us the benefit of their time and resources that it is impossible to thank everyone adequately.

With a few exceptions, we've changed the names of the students we discuss. Rebecca Miller, our case study in Chapter 7, is a composite of dozens of individual students Prosper coaches have worked with. We decided to build this case history around a composite character for two reasons. First, we did not want to compromise the privacy of any individual to the extent a case history of this detail would require. Second, coaching engagements are so highly individualized that the coaching ends up emphasizing one or more of the Six Prosperity Practices more than the others. We felt a case history based on a composite character would best fill the need for balance.

We also owe our gratitude to the many people who have read and re-read this book, offered comments, and voiced criticisms. Their suggestions helped make this book a reality.

Without a doubt, we could not have developed this book without our dedicated employees at Prosper. We have been inspired by their passion and drive to help people realize their true potential and live a better life. Together, we are working toward achieving true prosperity.

We'd especially like to thank the following individuals.

John Kador kept pushing us for the right words and the right idea to help us better communicate the concepts in this book; his skills in organization and vision are astounding. John was the perfect person to help us complete this project about prosperity because he lives it. Steve Piersanti's editorial skills are unmatched in the publishing industry, and his friendship we deeply cherish. Without Steve's guidance, this book would be twice as long and half as good.

We also value our association with the members of the remarkable Berrett-Koehler community, and we thank you all. We'd especially like to thank Jeevan Sivasubramaniam, Jaime Smith, Katie Sheehan, Kristen Frantz, David Marshall, Dianne Platner, Rick Wilson, Zoe Mackey, Mike Crowley, Bonnie Kaufman, Marina Cook, Cynthia Shannon, Catherine Lengronne, and Maria Jesus Aguilo. All of you acted as our brain trust; offering critical feedback and giving freely of yourselves. You are all an outstanding publishing crew to associate with.

At Prosper, we are especially grateful for the passion and dedication of Larissa Hommes, Jeff Kempton, Dane Ing, Kim Cannon, Jason Coulam, Aaron Peterson, Jade Koyle, Neal Jenks, and Michelle Zundel. Busy people all, they were with us every step of the way; from the book's design stages to its final completion. Without their assistance we would not have this book.

We would also like to thanks our mentors, friends, and other influencers in our lives who have helped shaped our lives for the better. Ken Blanchard, Vic Conant, Harvey Mackay, Kim Clark, Lynda Applegate, Cynthia Montgomery, Deepak Malhotra, Robert Allen, Tom Painter, Joe Vitale, Larry Benet, Alex Mandossian, Kevin Small, Kevin Hall, Ceasar Milder, Jose Fabricio, Mark Peterson, Chris Waters, Daniel McNairy, Neel Reddy, Vince Silva, Richard Andrews, Martha Lawrence, Paul Mix, Josh Christopherson, McKay Ercanbrack, Dave Greene, Steve Gross, Don Hutson, Cecily Markland, Brian Blair, Brandon Williams, Kevin Miyasaki, Justin Hyde, Clayton Christensen, Jay Abraham, Ned Hallowell, Jess Brown, Robin Bergstrom, Joe Soto, Joe Polish, Rudy Ruettiger, Paul Zane Pilzer, Mike Willbond, Robert Tingey, Devin Willis, Triton Willis, Damon Willis, Brent and Phelicia Hatch, Chloe Willis, Stan Sadowski, Farshad Fardad, and the Harvard OPM 39 group.

Ethan would like to thank his wonderful wife Ashley and their children Isabel, Ava, Gavin, Kate, and Ruby.

Randy would like to thank his wonderful wife Chai and their beautiful daughters Grace, Halle, Jane, and Sadie.

Most of our success in life is because of their unconditional love and support. We're also grateful to our parents for their loving direction in life: the late Donald Willis, Karen Willis-Hollcraft, and Dr. Richard Hollcraft, and Geedus Garn and Joan Garn. Together we've had a wonderful journey, and together we've set a course for lasting prosperity.

INDEX

ABOUT PROSPER

We are a leading provider in the world of one-to-one personalized education and mentoring for entrepreneurship, career development, stock market investing, real estate investing, personal development, personal finance, and e-commerce.

Learn more at www.prospering.com.

Entrepreneurship. Core Lesson Topics include Develop Business Strategies, Conduct Market Research, Perform Marketing Activities, Manage the Numbers, Manage Customer Service, Perform Employee Administration, Perform Administrative Tasks, Manage Websites and Technology, and Manage Personal Development.

Career Development. Core Lesson Topics include Resume Strategies, Negotiation, Interviewing, Time Management, Multi-Tasking vs. Focus, Building Effective Teams, Business Communication, Goal-Setting, Diversity in the Workplace, Being Indispensable, Leadership, Being Customer-Oriented, Building Culture, Strategies for Career Success, and Raises and Promotions.

Stock Market Investing. Core Lesson Topics include Market Basics, Fundamental Analysis, Technical Analysis, Sector Rotation, Volatility, Exchange Traded Funds, Debit Spreads, and Credit Spreads.

Real Estate Investing. Core Lesson Topics include Building a Solid Foundation, Strategic Planning, Finding Potential Deals, Analyzing Your Opportunities, Making an Offer, Funding Your Deals, Managing Your Property Effectively, Protecting your Assets, and Preparing for Closing.

Personal Development. Core Lesson Topics include The Ultimate You, Passion, Your Development Framework, Visualizing and Mapping Out Your Success, Developing You and Your Relationships, Taking Inventory of Potential Skills, Leveraging Your Network, and Celebrating Success.

Personal Finance. Core Lesson Topics include Introduction to Financial Planning, Cash Flow Management, Credit Management, Debt Elimination, Vision and Goal Setting, Risk Management, Retirement Planning, and Estate Planning.

E-Commerce. Core Lesson Topics include Starting an Online Business, Business Planning and Product Sourcing, Developing Your Own Website, Website Differentiation Growth, Generating Targeted Traffic 101, Developing a Social Media Strategy, and Managing Business Finances.

Students enjoy access to our online Success Center, elective classes, course curriculum, graduate group coaching sessions, and the Prosper E-Library.

We live by the philosophy *Your Life Is Your Business, Making It Prosper Is Ours*. With a personal mentor, Prosper enables the individual to make the jump from learning to earning in a remarkable way. We've helped over 75,000 individuals in over eighty countries find lasting prosperity through our programs.

We take pride in fulfilling our promises to our customers. Since our doors first opened in 1999, Prosper's customer experience has yielded significant returns, both to our students and to our coaches. Recent graduates have awarded Prosper high marks in customer satisfaction. We've also seen an average of more than 80 percent of our students graduate from our programs.

Before we partner with industry experts, we make sure they adhere to the highest ethical standards and conduct and that they are well recognized within their own industry. Our certified educational partners include Robert Allen, David Bach, Ken Blanchard, Adam Mesh, Harvey Mackay, Nightingale Conant, Donald Trump, John Assaraf, Jay Abraham, Joe Vitale, Stephen Cooper, Stephen Pierce, Andrew Daniels, Jason Lavigne, John Cummuta, and many others.

Prosper is a member of the Alliance for Lifelong Learning and has been accredited through Accrediting Commission International. Various recognitions include: Ernst & Young Entrepreneur of the Year, Stevie Finalist American Business Award for Best Overall Company, and the Best of Business Award from the Education Services and Small Business Commerce Association.

Among the many things we love about what we do as a company is that we give hope and purpose to our students. The Prosper team is composed of passionate, caring, and driven people who feel that helping people prosper is what business is all about.

To learn more about Prosper, visit us at www.prospering.com, or call us toll free at 1-800-370-4603.

ABOUT THE AUTHORS

ETHAN WILLIS
Chief Executive Officer
Co-Founder, Prosper
http://www.prospering.com

Ethan Willis is one of the founding partners of Prosper. He's served as the company's CEO since its inception in 1999. Under his leadership, Prosper has mentored over 75,000 students in over eighty countries.

Ethan coauthored the #1 *Wall Street Journal* and *New York Times* business bestselling book *The One Minute Entrepreneur* with his friend and mentor Ken Blanchard and with Don Hutson. He is passionate about entrepreneurship, has founded or cofounded six businesses in the past twelve years, and has employed over 2,000 people during that span.

Ethan has been recognized as Entrepreneur of the Year by Ernst and Young and a Top 100 Entrepreneur by Vspring, and his companies have been recognized as one of the best places to work in Utah. Ethan's work in the field of entrepreneurship has been published in *Business Week, USA Today,* Fox News, and various other publications. He is a graduate of Brigham Young University and the Owner President Management Program at Harvard University and is an alumnus of the Harvard Business School.

Ethan and his wife Ashley have five wonderful and active children they thoroughly enjoy.

RANDY GARN
Chief Relations Officer
Co-Founder, Prosper
http://www.prospering.com

Randy Garn is one of the founding partners of Prosper. He currently oversees all Business Development and works closely with some of the world's most renowned educators, speakers, and thought leaders.

Randy is a passionate networker and entrepreneur, and he loves growing companies and helping companies succeed. Randy's a serial entrepreneur in connection with Prosper. Randy has founded several other companies, which are industry leaders in online marketing specializing in customer acquisition, marketing, and product development. One of these companies, AdCafé.com, has more than 2 million subscribers and growing.

He was awarded Entrepreneur of the Year by Ernst and Young, was a Top 40 under 40 Entrepreneur, and has helped the company receive various awards in social and charitable involvement. Randy is an alumnus of Brigham Young University, a graduate of the Owner President Management Program at Harvard University, and an alumnus of the Harvard Business School.

Randy lives in Utah with his wife Char and their four beautiful daughters.

Berrett–Koehler
Publishers

Berrett-Koehler is an independent publisher dedicated to an ambitious mission: *Creating a World That Works for All*.

We believe that to truly create a better world, action is needed at all levels—individual, organizational, and societal. At the individual level, our publications help people align their lives with their values and with their aspirations for a better world. At the organizational level, our publications promote progressive leadership and management practices, socially responsible approaches to business, and humane and effective organizations. At the societal level, our publications advance social and economic justice, shared prosperity, sustainability, and new solutions to national and global issues.

A major theme of our publications is "Opening Up New Space." Berrett-Koehler titles challenge conventional thinking, introduce new ideas, and foster positive change. Their common quest is changing the underlying beliefs, mindsets, institutions, and structures that keep generating the same cycles of problems, no matter who our leaders are or what improvement programs we adopt.

We strive to practice what we preach—to operate our publishing company in line with the ideas in our books. At the core of our approach is stewardship, which we define as a deep sense of responsibility to administer the company for the benefit of all of our "stakeholder" groups: authors, customers, employees, investors, service providers, and the communities and environment around us.

We are grateful to the thousands of readers, authors, and other friends of the company who consider themselves to be part of the "BK Community." We hope that you, too, will join us in our mission.

A BK Life Book

This book is part of our BK Life series. BK Life books change people's lives. They help individuals improve their lives in ways that are beneficial for the families, organizations, communities, nations, and world in which they live and work. To find out more, visit **www.bk-life.com**.

Berrett–Koehler
Publishers

A community dedicated to creating
a world that works for all

Visit Our Website: www.bkconnection.com

Read book excerpts, see author videos and Internet movies, read
our authors' blogs, join discussion groups, download book apps, find
out about the BK Affiliate Network, browse subject-area libraries of
books, get special discounts, and more!

Subscribe to Our Free E-Newsletter, the *BK Communiqué*

Be the first to hear about new publications, special discount offers,
exclusive articles, news about bestsellers, and more! Get on the list
for our free e-newsletter by going to **www.bkconnection.com**.

Get Quantity Discounts

Berrett-Koehler books are available at quantity discounts for orders
of ten or more copies. Please call us toll-free at (800) 929-2929 or
email us at bkp.orders@aidcvt.com.

Join the BK Community

BKcommunity.com is a virtual meeting place where people from
around the world can engage with kindred spirits to create a world
that works for all. BKcommunity.com members may create their own
profiles, blog, start and participate in forums and discussion groups,
post photos and videos, answer surveys, announce and register for
upcoming events, and chat with others online in real time. Please join
the conversation!